SOOTHING NEWBORN BABIES

THREE NEWBORN PARENTING STRATEGIES TO SOOTHE SICK BABIES, SLEEP DEPRIVATION AND TEETHING DURING BABY'S FIRST YEAR

NONNA KNOWS BEST

CONTENTS

A SPECIAL GIFT TO OUR READERS

Thank you for taking the time to read my book. In appreciation to you I would love to give you a FREE Gift , my page, 5 Secrets You Didn't Know Could Boost Your Child's Intelligence at nonnaknowsbest.com

INTRODUCTION

"It is a smile of a baby that makes life worth living."

— DEBASISH MRIDHA

You can never be too prepared for parenthood. No matter how much research you've done, or how many babies you've babysat, nothing ever fully prepares you for the moment when your new child is placed in your arms. You might have learned how to change a diaper or to prepare a bottle. You might know all the rules and safety precautions, but every baby is different. Some babies are calm and content. Other babies are fussier. No matter what your baby's personality is, though, there is no one better suited to taking care of all of his or her needs than *you!*

It might not feel that way when you first hold your baby and feel entirely clueless, but don't worry! You'll learn before you know it, and reading this book is a great first step! Babies aren't as complicated as people make them out to be and by following my three simple rules of contentment for babies, you'll be able to meet their needs before you know it.

In my personal experience with my many siblings, children, and grandchildren, calming a baby is simple if you remember my Three C's of Contentment:

- Closeness
- Consistency
- Cues

Your baby is brand new in the world and is trusting you to help make all of the discomforts of the world go away. In the womb, your baby was kept warm and safe. There was no feeling of hunger or a wet diaper to be uncomfortable. There were the constant shushing sounds of the mother's heartbeat as the baby was swayed and rocked by her movement. Growing up inside the womb was the safest, most comfortable place your baby could have been, and compared to it, the world we are in is uncomfortable, scary, cold, and wet. Your baby needs your help to cope, and the best way you can do so is by learning to meet your baby's needs by following the three Cs.

Closeness

One of the best ways that you can help calm and soothe your baby is by keeping him close to you. Within the womb, your baby hears the sound of his mother's heartbeat constantly, and by holding your baby to your chest, he can hear yours as well. The familiar, rhythmic sound will help him to feel comfortable and secure.

Skin-to-skin care, in which your baby is placed on your bare chest (for moms and dads), is a wonderful way to facilitate bonding, regulate your baby's mood, and soothe him. When going shirtless is not an option, holding your baby close, such as in a baby sling or baby carrier, is the perfect way to help keep him calm.

I always recommend new parents focus on using a baby carrier instead of letting them sit in cribs, chairs, swings, and other baby holding devices. Babies depend on their parents for everything, so they're biologically designed to crave closeness with their caregivers. In many cultures, having babies strapped to the body is normal while mothers go about their daily chores, and those babies are often some of the happiest there are.

Attachment parenting refers to the parenting style in which the baby is taken care of closely.

Some of the key principles include:

- Being sensitive and responsive to your child's needs

- Bonding through touch
- Co-sleeping (more on this later, as co-sleeping and bed-sharing are different)
- Gentle parenting
- Being present emotionally
- Balancing your needs with your baby's

By meeting your baby's needs carefully through attachment parenting, you'll be able to meet the first of my three Cs.

Consistency

The second C is consistency. Babies and young children alike require consistency in order to feel confident. Consistency equals predictability and predictability makes for happy babies. Predictability teaches your baby what to expect and what will come next. Even young babies are able to notice a change to their routines, such as being out past bedtime, missing a feeding, or another caregiver. In consistency, babies can thrive because they feel emotionally secure. When they know what comes next, they will be more trusting and develop secure attachments to their caregivers.

Consistency in parenting has a few essential elements, including:

- **Regularity and predictability:** Babies who grow up in a predictable world recognize that they can trust their caregivers to meet their needs. They develop a better sense of security when their needs are met as necessary. Older children may be able to tolerate waiting for their needs to be met to some degree, but infants expect to be catered to immediately.

- **Schedules and routines:** Schedules and routines allow for predictability and stability. When your child can count on knowing that after bath comes storytime, followed by a feeding, gentle tooth or gum cleaning, and bed, they will naturally expect that every time. You might even notice resistance if you try to skip one part of the routine. Your baby might not be able to verbalize to you or understand what you explain to her, but she will be able to predict what will come next as she learns about the world around her.

- **Flexibility:** While stability is essential, your child still needs some degree of flexibility. This might look like reading different bedtime stories each night or playing different games and singing different songs. As long as needs are met and you follow a general schedule, your baby will feel secure, and flexibility will help your child learn to adapt to her surroundings.

- **Orderliness:** When you establish an orderly environment, your child will know what to expect while also feeling both secure and in control. You might not think of a baby as having any significant control over his environment, but he does learn from an early age. By the age of one, he may be putting toys in their bins after he finishes playing with them if you've taught him that that's where they belong. Your child will learn from you, so modeling orderliness now for your baby means that you'll also teach your child that it's important for him to be orderly as well.

Cues

Finally, the last of my Three Cs of Contentment is cues. You might think that your baby should be on a strict schedule, eating only at set times, napping only at set times, and being changed only at set times, but let go of this notion. The truth is, your baby needs to be cared for with the understanding that your baby doesn't eat, sleep, and breathe like clockwork. Yes, there are usually patterns that you can follow to predict behaviors and needs, but that doesn't mean they'll always happen in that way.

Instead of watching the clock to know what to do for your baby, you need to listen to your baby's cues. As you learn your baby's cues, you'll understand when the problem is that she is fussy because her diaper is wet or because she's hungry. You'll be able to tell the difference between her being tired, bored, or sore because she's teething. You'll learn to recognize what she really needs.

Your baby's cues are primarily nonverbal at this age. Your baby will cry. But, rather than doing whatever you can to keep her from ever crying, remember that her cries are the only way she can communicate right now. She doesn't know how to tell you verbally that she's hungry or tired. There will be a time when she can, but for now, what she needs from you is for you to learn her cries. She'll learn to speak in time, but for now, it's best for you to pick up on her cues.

Responding to your baby's cues on demand is the most important part of parenting. As you soothe your baby, you meet your baby's needs. You bond with your baby. You also set up the foundation of healthy emotional development for later by teaching him how he can regulate his needs. There are several primary cues that you'll need to learn, including hunger, pain or discomfort, engagement, overstimulation, and sleepiness. These will vary a bit from baby to baby, but once you start picking up on how your baby communicates, you'll be meeting needs like a pro!

Hungry babies will usually give shorter, lower-pitched whimpers rather than piercing cries, unless you've missed the cue. They will also turn their heads toward their parent or caregiver, looking for food. They will suck on their fingers and fists or try to suck on the air. If you see these cues, and your baby woke up recently or has not eaten recently, there's a good chance that your baby is hungry.

Sometimes, your baby is hurting or uncomfortable. These cries are sudden and louder, lasting continuously. It could be that your baby is hot or cold, or wet. If you notice your baby tugging at her ears, she may have an ear infection or be teething. She may also have a soggy or soiled diaper, or suffer from a diaper rash. Or, if she's arching her back while crying, she may be suffering from acid reflux.

Sleepy babies are always a bit more difficult to catch onto, especially because there is only a short window of time to get your baby to sleep before he becomes a fussy, overtired mess who isn't likely to sleep very well. Look for signs such as yawning, turning away from you, and rubbing eyes that look like they're unfocused. He may be frowning or squirmier than usual because he wants to be put down to sleep.

Playful babies want to engage with you to learn. In fact, even just hours after birth, you can get your baby to copy you by sticking out your tongue. Babies learn through all of their interactions with you, so you don't want to miss out on this period of time! The more that you can catch onto these cues, the better.

You may notice that your baby is watching you closely, or that she is attempting to reach or turn toward you. By just 3 months of age, she may be attempting to mimic the pitch of your voice, and by 6 months of age, she'll be making consonant sounds ("ba ba ba" or "na na na"). She may blow raspberries and look interested in everything around her as well. She wants to play with you!

Overstimulated babies need a break. They can only handle so much stimulation before they feel stressed out and upset about what's around them. They need to be free to take a break, and that means reading your baby's disengagement cues. These include looking away and refusing to make eye contact, pushing their hands out to push away from you, or squirming and kicking. Your baby needs some time to cool off and if you ignore them, you're likely to get an agitated, fussy baby that seems inconsolable. Really, he just needs a little break and maybe a nap.

Soothing your baby might seem difficult at first, but as you get to know what the most common cues are, you should be able to recognize what your baby's needs are. If you can follow the three Cs, remembering closeness, consistency, and cues, you'll have a happier baby. A happy baby is a cared-for baby, so by learning the best way to do so, you're learning how to best treat your baby!

As you read, you'll learn how to take care of your baby's most important needs to keep her safe. You'll learn about babyproofing, general care for your child, and more. You'll discover how to recognize changes to your baby's sleep and how to manage it. You will learn about feeding choices and changes your baby will go through over the next several months. You'll be introduced to some of the most common cues and illness concerns that parents have during infancy, and how to cope with teething, grumpy babies.

Babies love me. My children and their spouses have taken to calling me the "Baby Whisperer" because I've always been able to pick up my grandchildren and soothe them quickly. They all ask me what my secret is, and the answer? There is no secret! I'm not doing anything special!

When you hold your baby, swaddle and comfort them. Talk to them gently and smile. They have the same needs as you do: to feel loved and secure, and I've learned to give that security to the babies I hold and care for. There's nothing special about what I do with my grandbabies. Anyone can learn to do what I do! And it all begins with those three Cs.

Remember that the days with your infant may seem long, but those years are oh-so-short. Before you know it, you will blink and your tiny newborn will be a toddler, in school, and leaving the nest. Each of those long days that you have, even when your precious baby is bawling in your arms, is a blessing. It's a beautiful time in your life, and it will be over before you know it.

By using these tools, you'll be able to take out much of the stress of childrearing and spend more time marveling at the little life in your arms.

CHAPTER 1 - PROTECTING YOUR NEWBORN AND PREVENTING INJURIES

Everyone tells you that the moment you lay eyes on your newborn, all of the struggles will melt away. It won't matter how hard bringing that baby into the world was, or how long or hard the adoption process was. In that moment, when you first hold your baby in your arms, everything feels right.

And yet, as soon as your baby is born, you have the realization that things aren't easy anymore. Before the baby was in the world, protecting him or her was far easier. Now, your baby is exposed to the real world and learning the sensation of hunger, pain, and cold for the first time. Everything is new and your baby is exposed to everything.

It's normal to feel a bit scared of what the world will have in store for your precious little bundle of joy, but thankfully, there are steps that you can take to protect your child. There are ways that you can help keep the environment your child is in as safe as possible. From regulating visitors to making sure that your pet is introduced to your baby in a safe manner, there are ways that you can help to ensure that your baby's first year is as smooth as possible.

It's okay to feel lost during these times. Between the lack of sleep, the sudden shift in the dynamics in your household, and the welcoming of a brand new addition to your family, it's easy to be overwhelmed. Though childbirth is natural, babies don't come with instructions and you'll have to learn to navigate caring for your own. Thankfully, you don't have to do it on your own. There is a plethora of knowledge available online for your perusal and as you read through this chapter, you'll be introduced to everything that you need to know right out of the hospital.

Room Temperature for Your Baby

You might be worried that your baby will be too cold if you have air conditioning running or too hot if the heater runs in the winter. Babies, like older children, usually do just fine in temperatures between 65 and 68 degrees Fahrenheit, given that they're over 5 pounds. Any smaller, and they will struggle to retain their heat.

Smaller babies will usually have a harder time regulating their temperatures. Rely on layers of clothing to keep your child comfortable. Place your baby somewhere without hot or cold drafts, and for very small babies, skin-to-skin contact, sometimes called kangaroo care, is the best way to regulate temperature.

Take extra care in colder weather, as during this time, outdoor air has little moisture, and when it is warmed up indoors, it sucks all of the moisture from the nose and skin, which can cause dry skin and dried mucus to build up in the nose. Dried mucus in the nose can interfere with breathing and may lower resistance to infection and illness. Humidifiers can be perfect in the winter months to keep your baby comfortable and breathing easily.

Make sure that you resist the urge to overdress your child, especially in the winter. Keeping the room too hot, with the baby all bundled up can make him or her uncomfortable, and even cause the development of heat rash.

Visitors

Baby coming into the world is a time of great joy for many people in their inner circles. Your friends, family, coworkers, friends of family, neighbors, and even acquaintances may want to stop by in those early days to meet your new arrival. Of course, this doesn't mean that you have to allow a carousel of people to parade in and out of your home for those six weeks. Babies don't spoil after the newborn period and you are allowed to tell people that you're not up for a visit without owing them an explanation.

Let other people know when it works for you and how much time you've got available to visit, even if that time is none at all sometimes (especially if Mom wants the first week or two to recover physically). Delivering a baby is hard work and those first precious days are gone before you know it.

When you do have visitors, your rules are law. Insist on anyone who is ill or may have been exposed to an illness stay home, as babies do not have a functional immune system in those earliest days, and getting sick in those days can be dangerous. Ask all visitors to wash their hands before holding the baby.

As an added help, if you do feel comfortable having other people in your home right after the birth, consider letting trusted visitors care for the baby if you need a bit of a break. No one's faulting you for needing thirty minutes to shower or enjoy a hot cup of coffee. If you're comfortable and you trust them, this can be a great way to get some extra rest.

Bringing Baby Home to a Pet

If you have a pet at home, you may be wondering how they will react when suddenly, they don't get all of your attention anymore. Will they be jealous? Will they try to hurt your baby? There's a chance that something might happen, as both babies and pets are unpredictable, especially as Baby becomes mobile, but with some simple considerations, you can make sure that your transition is smooth. Keep in mind that this time is a major adjustment for your pet as well.

When you're in the hospital, have someone bring a blanket with your baby's scent on it home to the pet so they can start getting used to the smell before the baby is there. Babies smell a lot different from adults, and that way, the smell of your little one isn't completely foreign when you bring your bundle of joy through the door for the first time.

When your baby is at home, keep in mind that it will take three weeks, or more, for your pet to adapt. They may have dramatically different reactions. Some may be curious about the baby, or even affectionate and protective. Others will completely ignore the presence.

No matter what the reaction is, it's important that, especially at first, you never leave your pet alone with your baby. You don't want a well-meaning dog to knock the baby over or a cat to decide that Baby's chest is a cozy bed.

Even when you are supervising, make sure that you avoid situations that may cause your animal to make sudden, unexpected movements or noises. You want your pet to be kept at a distance from your baby, who may grasp onto your pet's fur.

Remember that your pet isn't much different than your baby, and you will need to have some compassion for your pets during this transition. Remembering to treat them with kindness is more likely to encourage them to feel comfortable around Baby. Otherwise, they could make a connection that the presence of your baby means they don't get their most valuable resource: you! Make sure your animals still get plenty of love too.

Handling a Newborn

If you've never taken care of a newborn before, you're probably afraid of hurting them. Their necks are floppy. They can't really hold themselves up or reposition themselves if they're uncomfortable. They are entirely reliant on you for everything other than being able to breathe!

You may be afraid that you'll do something that will hurt them, but remember this: babies are resilient. It would take a lot to do serious harm to a baby, and the likelihood of that happening in an accident is slim. Take a deep breath, relax, and enjoy your baby.

If you want to know some general guidelines, follow these next rules for making sure that your baby is kept safe.

Wash Hands

Your newborn doesn't have much in the way of a functional immune system. If he or she is breastfed, they will get the benefit of antibodies passed through milk. However, it's still good common practice to wash your hands in warm water or use sanitizer before touching your babies. Make sure that everyone has clean hands before touching babies.

Support Baby's Head

The biggest mistake that people make when holding a newborn baby for the first time is not supporting the baby's head. Your baby's neck isn't strong enough to support itself yet, so you must

carry the baby with support. When you lay down the baby, always keep your hand on the back of his or her neck to support the neck, and also support it when holding the baby upright.

Never Shake Your Newborn

Rocking babies is supposed to be a surefire way of calming them down, but when that rocking gets too rough it can be harmful. No matter how frustrated you get, shaking your baby is *never* an option. Shaking can cause internal bleeding and irreparable brain damage, or even death in serious cases. Your baby is still too delicate as a newborn to be bounced on a knee or tossed into the air.

Always Check Restraints in Strollers, Car Seats, and Carriers

Before you move your child in a car seat, carrier, or stroller, make sure they are buckled in according to the manufacturer's requirements. These may vary from country to country. Countries like the United States have chest buckles that cross right across the breastbone, while other countries may commonly use seats where the buckle and five points of the harness connect near the pelvis. Make sure that you always use all the buckles and that you follow manufacturer instructions to ensure that your baby is kept safe.

Clothing Guide

More often than not, babies are overdressed instead of under-dressed, which is unhealthy for the baby. Generally speaking, it's better to underdress and correct if your baby looks too cold or uncomfortable instead of overdressing them. Most babies naturally have cold hands, even when they're warm enough.

Instead, go by the temperature of the neck or arms. If the arms or neck are warm, the baby is probably at a comfortable temperature. You can also tell by the color of your baby's cheeks. Babies who are too warm will be flushed while those that are cold may lose color and fuss.

In winter months or cold weather, use a warm cap to retain heat in the head. Most of the baby's body heat will be lost through the head, so it's essential that you cover it up. However, if your baby is sleeping, make sure that they don't have a hat on, as it could slip and pose a suffocation risk.

To pull on sweaters and shirts with smaller openings, you want to start at the back of the head, then pull over the head and forward, carefully stretching it so you can pass it over the head and nose. Then, you can slide the baby's arms into the sleeves. To remove, you do the reverse; pull out the baby's arms, then carefully lift the sweater up and over the head, pulling gently to the back.

Preventing Injuries at Home

Are you one of those parents who believe that everything around is potentially a death trap, or the one who believes that your child will be fine without any need for childproofing? The best thing you can do is make sure that you fall somewhere in the middle. You can't be too overprotective, but you also have to make sure that you're there to guide them.

While thinking that statistically, your child will be fine is true, why take the chance with your beautiful baby? Make sure that you're protecting your child by childproofing appropriately, but without going overboard. Finding that middle ground is essential if you want to raise happy, healthy, and resilient children.

Babies are naturally curious and they're quick. They're going to be hurt at some point, no matter how hard you try to keep them safe. You might think that there's no way they're able to roll when you leave them on the bed and turn your back, but then... *THUNK.* Baby somehow rolled for the first time and fell off the bed. It happens more than any parent wants to admit.

While you can't prevent every injury, you can certainly take precautions against the most dangerous situations that are the most likely to hurt them. Even just protecting against the riskiest of occurrences will do your child a world of benefit.

Making Home Sweet Home a Safe Haven

Your baby may not be mobile when you first bring him or her home, but before you know it, that tiny, helpless bundle will be rolling, crawling, toddling, and running through your home. Within that year, your baby can and most likely will try to get their hands on every little thing possible. They'll be desperate to get their hands on whatever they can reach to start learning about the world around them. That means that yes, you'll need to protect your valuable belongings, but the most valuable of all is your baby!

Anything dangerous should be put away or protected against. This means electrical outlets should be covered, choking hazards should be put away, there won't be access to trash or electronics, and more. You might think that those babyproofing kits online are overkill, but does it really hurt to put that cabinet lock and toilet seat lock on? Is it really that bad to put up a gate around the fireplace to make sure that your child can't reach it? When babyproofing, take the position of it's always better to be overprepared than underprepared. Sure, that gate might have been unnecessary, but what if you hadn't put it up and Baby found a way to get hurt?

Make sure that you start the babyproofing process before your baby needs it. The sooner, the better! You may want to set up the babyproofing process before you even bring the baby home. Safety should always be a priority.

Likewise, you can't ever assume that your home is safe enough. There's always something that you can do to make it safer. But remember, a babyproofed home still isn't a substitute for supervision. You should always make sure that you watch your baby. Even if you think that your home is safe, there's probably something that Baby can get into.

To babyproof, follow these guides:

The Floor

Start with getting down on the floor at a baby's level and look around. What can you see?

Make sure you:

- Move any choking hazards.
- Move all houseplants.
- Make sure there are no litter boxes, trash cans, or other waste available for your baby toreach.
- Make sure your baby can't get underneath any furniture.
- Block off fireplaces, wood stoves, and heaters.
- Put pads on furniture with sharp edges, such as coffee tables, entertainment stands, chairs, and other hard edges.
- Put baby gates on stairs, using only gates that are screwed in rather than pressure gates, which could slip.

- Cover up railings around a landing that a baby could fall through.
- Make sure no carpet is loose.

The House

- Cover all electrical outlets or replace them with covers that automatically close over outlets.
- Make sure all electrical cords are out of reach.
- Lock all drawers, cabinets, and toilets.
- Identify which tables and chairs may be off-balance and tip if Baby uses them as edges to pull up on.
- Put away tablecloths.
- Make sure all top-heavy furniture is strapped to the wall. Pay special attention to dressers and bookcases. Use earthquake straps to do so.
- Secure the TV either to the wall or to the entertainment stand it is on to prevent it from falling.
- Replace door stops with rubber stoppers
- Keep all furniture away from windows to prevent babies from leaning too far out or falling.
- Keep cord blinds up and out of reach at all times. They are a serious strangulation risk.
- Reduce the water heater down to 120 degrees F to prevent accidental scalds.Never hold your baby while cooking or while drinking hot coffee. It's not worth the risk of serious injury or burn!

Babyproofing Appliances

- Use appliance locks to keep the oven and refrigerator closed. If you have a stove with knobs on the front to adjust the temperature or turn on the stove, consider getting babyproofing covers to keep Baby from being able to turn on the gas.
- Get covers for burners.
- Double-check that the garage door will bounce up if it comes into contact with anything to prevent it from crushing someone. Test this with a garbage can. The garage door should go back up without damaging the can.

Environmental Hazards

- Make sure all hazardous chemicals are kept locked in a cabinet, including your daily cleaners.
- Make sure that smoke detectors are in good condition. There should be at least one on every floor in the home, and preferably, one in each room. Make sure that batteries are changed annually.
- Install carbon monoxide detectors on every floor in your home.
- Double-check all paint in your home is lead-free. This is especially important for you to check in older homes.

- Keep toiletries and medication out of reach and locked away.

Checking for Choking Hazards

Babies are quick to pop just about anything into their mouths, which means it's your duty to make sure that there is nothing available to them that they could choke on. Babies, in these earliest stages, aren't all that great at using their hands, so they're quick to put things in their mouths to explore them instead. The oral fixation can continue until the baby is almost three years old, though it commonly ends by the second year.

While babyproofing is a good start, it's a good idea to make sure that you're taking extra precautions as well, such as making sure that you're cutting up the food appropriately and that you're prepared to perform the Heimlich maneuver if necessary.

Choking Hazards

Some foods are riskier than others, especially for younger children. There are several foods that are known to be choking hazards, which must either be cut or withheld until the child is older. This include:

- Hot dogs (cut them into half-circles)
- Grapes (cut into four wedges per grape)
- Raisins (wait until your child is older)
- Nuts (wait until your child is older)

- Firm foods in chunks (cheese, veggies, meats, fruits; cut into manageable bite-sized bits)
- Hard candies (wait until later, including lollipops)
- Popcorn (wait until your child is older)
- Sticky foods (avoid things like peanut butter or marshmallows)

Keeping Baby Safe

To keep your baby safe when eating, consider the following:

- Always cut firm foods into small pieces.
- Cut round foods into quarters or strips before providing them to Baby
- Pace eating speeds so Baby's mouth isn't full of food.
- Avoid sticky and hard foods until later.
- Keep your baby sitting upright when eating.

Heimlich Maneuver

If there is ever a moment when your baby does choke, call 911 immediately for further instructions and help. In the meantime, make sure that you also know the Heimlich maneuver to help clear the airway while you wait for paramedics to arrive.

1. Put the baby face-down on your forearm, using your hand to support her neck and head.

2. Hit the baby five times in between the shoulder blades to try to dislodge the food.

3. If this doesn't work to dislodge the food, turn the baby over and center your index and middle fingers in the center of the baby's chest, between the nipples.

4. Use your fingers to give five quick chest thrusts to dislodge the food.

5. Repeat until you dislodge the food or paramedics arrive.

Eradicating Other Hazards

There are certain choking hazards that should always be kept out of reach of Baby. Before you ever let your baby down to play, make sure that you double-check for any of the following:

- Coins
- Buttons
- Batteries
- Toys with small pieces
- Raisins
- Paper clips
- Compressing toys (balloons or foam balls)
- Bottle caps
- Pen caps
- Thumbtacks

Pet and Baby Safety

Your pet may not be happy that you've brought a baby home. Your pet may be depressed, aggressive, or snappy. It's right to be concerned about this, and to think twice about whether you'd like your baby to be alone with your pet. Remember that your pet may not be as kind as you'd hope, so you should never trust your unpredictable animal alone with your baby.

Your pet may see the baby as a strange thing that is loud, smelly, and demanding all of your attention, all of which could be threatening, or even distressing in certain situations. Make sure that you are always between your baby and pet. This continues even as your baby grows. Infants and toddlers aren't known for being friendly to pets who they want to play with and not all pets will sit back and take the abuse; some may choose to snap instead to teach Baby their boundaries.

Sleep Safety

Your crib is meant to be safe and secure, but if you don't put it together, that safe haven could actually put your baby at risk of SIDS or suffocation. A lot of previously used equipment and guidelines no longer apply, so if you got your information from someone who has been out of the loop with baby safety for the last 20 years, they may not be a reliable source of information. Make sure your crib is ready for your baby by:

- Never use a crib built before 1992. They don't meet safety standards.
- Make sure the crib is still sturdy. Many times, cribs get passed from family member to family member, and this can cause them to lose integrity, especially in screws that have been used repeatedly. Don't try holding it together with glue or zip ties if you're missing a screw.
- Make sure all slats are less than 2 ⅜ inches apart. Otherwise, there could be a risk for Baby's head getting stuck.
- The mattress should be firm in the crib. You should be able to, at most, fit just one finger between the mattress and slat. Any more is too much and the baby could become stuck.
- Keep the crib away from windows or dangling things that could become a strangulation risk.
- Hang the mobile somewhere Baby can't reach, and once your baby can pull up and reach for it, it's time to take it down.
- If you use a bumper pad, make sure it is a ventilated one, otherwise, the risk for suffocation goes up. Any bumper pads should be removed as soon as your baby starts pulling up.
- Make sure all paints and stains are safe for your baby. You might not realize it yet, but Baby will be a little beaver when their teeth start coming in. They'll chew

on anything, including the rail of their crib. Check the rail regularly for damage.

- Avoid corner posts on the cribs, which could be caught on your baby's clothing and pose a strangulation risk.

Hazards on the Go

As soon as you put your baby in the car, you might worry about a car accident. However, in most cases, a baby strapped into a car seat the right way will protect your precious bundle of joy from most injuries. Every car seat will come with a manual that is meant to tell you exactly how to safely install your car seat.

However, if you're not sure what you're doing, there are likely places in your community at the fire station, hospital, or police station where they can check on your handiwork and make sure that Baby's seat is nice and secure. Don't feel silly about this—many people install their car seats improperly and the only way to know for sure is to get it checked out.

Safety regulations are often changing with the times. Legally, children must ride in rear-facing seats until they are at least one year old *and* at least 20 lbs., but you are encouraged to rear-face as long as possible until your child outgrows it. Don't worry about complaints about feet being cramped; you won't get them! Babies and toddlers have flexible joints and are perfectly comfortable keeping their feet criss-cross while rear-facing.

Rear-facing as long as possible is highly encouraged, as no matter how big your baby may be on the outside, their bones are not yet fused enough to be able to withstand an accident while front-facing until they are much older. Younger children are at a higher risk for internal decapitation in an accident when seated in front-facing seats if they are too young.

Aiming for 4, if possible, keeps your child safe, and ideally, you would rear-face as long as you can before your child outgrows their seat's limits, which can be quite high these days. Some of the best affordable seats on the market support rear-facing until 50 lbs. and 49 inches tall, which would support even a 95th percentile boy at the age of 4.

You should try to never put Baby in the front seat while driving, especially if you cannot disable the passenger-side airbag. Baby belongs in the back seat, as the force of an airbag blowing could be potentially fatal in the car seat.

If your baby starts to cry, focus on driving. Don't reach back or try to fix the problem. If you're close to your destination, your baby will be fine crying for the next few minutes. If you can't handle it, there's nothing wrong with stopping for a few minutes to tend to Baby's needs before getting back on the road. No multitasking!

Make sure that Baby is always wearing the harness in the car seat correctly. They should be tight enough so that the baby isn't tossed out of the seat. You shouldn't be able to pinch any slack with the straps and the harness clip should sit across the chest. It's okay to be able to slide a finger between your baby and the clip, but not much more.

Don't be fooled by puffy coats or snowsuits either. While the harness may seem tight with the puffy coat on, it's not actually enough to keep the baby in the seat in the event of an accident. None of the layers your child is wearing should be able to be compressed significantly when riding in the car. Instead, use fleece jackets and pants with a blanket to keep your baby warm. It's safer.

Again: Never Shake a Baby!

Babies cry *a lot*. It can be overwhelming if you can't get him or her to quiet down, but no matter how angry or frustrated you get, you can *never* shake a baby. Shaken baby syndrome occurs when infants and young children are shaken violently. This movement can cause the brain to bounce around in the skull, or even sever the spinal cord, causing death or permanent severe brain damage.

Typically, it occurs because the parent or caregiver has reached the end of their rope and simply can't deal with the crying anymore. It's okay to be frustrated, but if you get to that point where you feel like you're going to snap, the best thing you can do is walk away.

Even if your baby is screaming, if there is nothing noticeably wrong, the baby is fed and clean, and you're just done trying, it's okay to put your baby in a safe space, such as the crib or a swing, and walk away for a little bit. Take a few minutes to calm yourself down. Step outside of your home and just give yourself a few minutes to unwind, get a snack, or do something else to quickly reset. Ten minutes of your baby crying is less harmful than you potentially harming your baby in the heat of the moment.

Choosing Your Baby's Doctor

You've got many different options for your baby's doctor. You should find the right one for your baby prior to giving birth, which might sound tricky, but it's good to have a game plan early on, especially because there are so many early doctor appointments.

Do you want a pediatrician, a family doctor, or a nurse practitioner? Nurse practitioners are registered nurses that have had extra training to be able to function as a doctor would in many situations. They're able to work with a doctor when necessary, but they can be great for preventative care. Any of the three options will be more than enough for your child's regular care.

When selecting a doctor, consider whether your child will have one doctor, or whether they may be rotated through, depending upon who is available at the time. It is important that you choose what you are most comfortable with; some parents prefer to have the same doctor each time while others may not care.

Schedule an initial appointment prior to the birth to get to know the pediatrician. Speak to them about concerns you might have, as well as some of your particular preferences. What do they think about vaccines? Breastfeeding? Will they make you feel judged if you tell them your sleeping arrangements? Do you feel comfortable with them in general? If you don't feel comfortable, there's no harm in finding one that works better for your family. 18 years is a long time to keep bringing your child in to see someone you don't trust or like.

Planning the Homecoming

The first few weeks after giving birth are difficult. However, with a bit of foresight, you can plan out that time well and help make that homecoming much easier to get through.

Arrange for Help

In the beginning, you're likely to be exhausted. If your baby's father is not available to help after the birth, regardless of the reason, or if both you and your baby's father are overwhelmed and don't know where to begin, you may want to arrange to have some sort of extra help in the beginning. This could look like having someone stay to take some of the overnight care off of Mom and Dad during those first few weeks, or it could be having someone arrange a meal train, or cleaning up the house for your new family.

If you don't have a community of people nearby, you may even consider hiring a housekeeper, doula, or mother's helper to keep up with the work.

Nurse Home Visits

Some hospitals will offer nurse home visits a few days after the birth of your child, especially if your stay was less than 48 hours, to ensure that there are no medical conditions that may be popping up. They may also be able to assist with breastfeeding, if applicable.

Preparing Your Home

Before your child is born, it's a good idea to clean it up and prepare it. If you have a home from before 1980, it probably has lead paint, which you'll need to seal or have removed professionally. You may also want to check the basement and other damp areas for black mold to treat them if necessary. If you have a well, make sure that the water is safe, and discuss fluoride if necessary.

Moving Your Baby Around

Your baby is probably going to spend time all over the house with you. You'll have to move him or her from room to room as you go about your daily tasks. There are some ways that you can consider making this easier. Parents often turn to swings, seats, walkers, bouncers, jumpers, and more to keep their baby happy.

Choosing which options will work for you depends on your own thoughts and preferences.

Seats, Swings, and Walkers: When Should You Use Them?

As a note, baby walkers are no longer recommended. In fact, the American Academy of Pediatrics actively recommends avoiding the use of a walker, as they pose a serious risk to the baby's health and safety. Instead of providing a baby with a walker to move around, consider giving them a stationary jumper or activity center instead. They still have plenty of fun, but they can't roll their way into trouble.

Plastic baby seats have become somewhat outdated as well. While you can still find them on the market, now with additional straps for safety, they aren't particularly recommended, as the baby cannot move naturally. Rather than a plastic seat, consider a cloth sling or bouncer instead, which will allow for a normal range of motion. You may also choose to use a swing for comfort or to rock your child to sleep while you are busy.

Ideally, if possible, you use a cloth baby carrier, which you can attach to your chest or back. Using a chest carrier can be helpful for breastfeeding mothers as well, as they'll be able to put it on and carry their baby comfortably and nurse relatively easily while still having hands free.

Strollers, Carriages, and Carriers

Strollers are at a bit of an angle that's too much for babies who cannot yet hold their heads steadily. Ideally, newborns and young infants do much better in a baby carrier strapped to their parents' chest, where they can enjoy the closeness. However, you also have the option to have a dual travel system in which the car seat straps into the stroller and can be removed on the go, allowing you to go from car to stroller without waking up your baby.

You may also choose to use a carriage. Also known as a pram, these are seats that will work as a sort of portable bassinet, letting you walk with the baby laying down. However, unless you will be taking many long walks, they aren't really necessary when you could sooner use a baby carrier or a travel set.

When Baby gets too big for the baby carrier, you may also choose to use a backpack with a metal frame, seat, and straps to hold your baby in place on your shoulders. This new vantage point gives Baby lots to look at and keeps your hands free.

When to Expect Your Baby to Walk

One thing you're probably looking forward to is seeing your baby's first steps. There's a wide range of what is normal for babies. Some will skip crawling altogether. Others will take much longer to get off the floor and start toddling around.

Anything between 8 months and 18 months is still normal. They need to develop enough core strength in order to support their weight and control their limbs. Before your baby walks, they will probably cruise, or walk with help, such as while holding your hands or while clinging to furniture.

Toiletries and Medical Supplies

Your baby's skin is delicate, and it's understandable that you don't want to put just anything on it. As a general rule, you will want the following supplies on hand:

- Soap (any mild soap; some liquid soaps may cause irritation to the skin, but your baby probably won't need much soap until he or she is on the go)
- Baby oil (any baby oil should be fine for normal or dry skin)
- Lanolin and petrolatum (these are good to protect the skin when diaper rash flares up)
- Infant nail scissors (these are blunted to avoid accidents. The surest way to protect those little fingertips is with a nail file)
- Digital thermometer (go for a regular digital thermometer to boost accuracy)
- Nose syringe (good for removing mucus from the nose before Baby can blow it)

Bathing Your Baby

The first bath probably isn't going to be very fun, but after a few weeks, most babies come around. This time is great for enjoying together, and your baby will likely love splashing. The water should be warm, but not hot, and you want to keep the room warm as well.

Consider giving a bath before feeding because most babies will want to sleep after. Eventually, when your child begins eating three meals per day, you may want to shift to one bath a day in the evening, after dinner. You may also consider making this a part of a predictable bedtime routine.

Body Parts

Taking care of your baby comes with a lot of considerations that wouldn't matter for adults.

Many body parts are much more sensitive and must be protected and taken care of.

Skin

Many babies develop spots, splotches, and rashes early on in life. Most will fade away without concern, but it's always a good idea to check in with a doctor whenever you notice a new one.

Ears

The outer ear needs to be washed with a washcloth regularly. Don't use a cotton swab inside the ear.

Eyes

Baby eyes clean themselves with tears, so you don't need to do anything unless the eyes look irritated.

Nose

The nose will keep itself clean with mucus. You can wipe away any dried mucus with the corner of a washcloth to clean it away from the nose. If the nose is plugged up with dried mucus, you will need to clear it out with a nose suction piece.

Nails

Nails can be tricky; your baby is likely to pull away. However, you can trim them when your baby is sleeping, or make it a fun routine. Consider using a file so there are no sharp edges to the nails and no risk of hurting Baby's fingers.

Fontanel

Your baby has a soft spot on the top of his or her head. This is known as the fontanel. These close between the ages of 9 months and 2 years, though the average is between 12 and 18 months. Don't worry about hurting it; light, gentle touch isn't going to do anything.

Navel

The umbilical cord is clipped and cut shortly after birth. The stump will then be left to dry and fall off, which takes between 2 and 3 weeks. When it falls off, there will then be a raw spot left behind, which will take days to heal. This spot must be kept dry and clean. The scab will do well to protect it. Dry it well after bathtime, and don't be concerned by a drop or two of blood if the navel is pulled on by clothing.

Try to keep the diaper beneath the navel; you may notice that many newborn diapers actually have the top of the diaper cut to allow for this. Keeping the navel uncovered will help it to dry out and heal. If the skin surrounding the navel is red, smelly, or hot, you must take your baby to the doctor to ensure that the baby is treated.

The Penis

In boys, the penis has a large sleeve of skin, known as the foreskin. It covers the head of the penis, with enough of an opening to let out urine without risk of diaper rash. The skin will naturally separate after time, with most boys being able to pull it back by age 4, though it's not abnormal for the skin to remain fused until puberty.

White, waxy discharge at the tip is normal. This is smegma, created as a natural lubricant to protect the penis.

Circumcision

Though circumcision holds religious significance in Jewish and Muslim cultures, it is not required. Most doctors agree that for most people, there is no medical benefit to the surgery.

Penis Care

You may notice that your baby boy has an erection sometimes. This is normal, and may actually be a sign that he is about to urinate, so consider covering him up before a mess is made. There is nothing special that you have to do to take care of the penis. Simply wash it the way you would a finger. Do not retract foreskin if the baby is uncircumcised. This skin is sealed to the penis and it will tear if you forcibly retract it.

For circumcised babies, change his diaper often, while rubbing petroleum jelly or something similar to the wound to prevent the healing skin from sticking to the diaper.

Babies Thrive on Touch

Prior to birth, babies are kept within the bodies of their mothers. They are kept warm, listening to their mothers' heartbeats, feeling the movements, and being nourished as well. In many areas of the world, babies are kept against their mothers until they are much older in slings and other carriers. They are with their mothers for all activities, breastfed on demand, and get to spend their earliest years with their mother. These babies are happy.

Babies crave physical touch, and mothers crave giving it. Through physical touch, both the parent and baby's relaxation hormones are released. They are happier and pain is reduced. This is especially true for premature infants, who fare much better with daily skin-to-skin time. Kangaroo care and skin-to-skin time are crucial, not just for Mom, but also for Dad in those earliest days. Try to keep your baby as close to you as possible, especially in the earliest three months.

CHAPTER 2 - WHY IS YOUR BABY CRYING SO MUCH?

Babies are good at crying. Sometimes, it might even seem like all they ever do is cry. But this is for good reason: this is your child's main way to communicate! Your baby can't speak to you the way an older child can, so they cry. It doesn't only mean that your child is sad or hurt; it could also be that your child is hungry, tired, fussy, bored, or too warm or cold. It could be that your baby doesn't like something or someone, or your baby may simply want to go back to Mom or Dad.

In this chapter, we'll emphasize several of the most common reasons that babies cry. Often, it is something that you can do something about. Other times, it could be related to colic, which we will discuss as well. We will discuss how to treat a crying child, calming your child, and tips and tricks for those hard-to-soothe babies that seem quick to cry, even when nothing appears to be wrong.

What Does All That Crying Mean?

Your baby will cry. A lot. That's okay! This is just a part of having babies. As your baby grows up, the crying will fade away. In the first few weeks of parenthood, you probably have no idea whether the problem is a diaper, hunger, illness, or general fussiness. But, more often than not, your baby is crying because she is *tired*. We don't usually realize just how often babies sleep in the newborn days if we've never had a newborn before.

Other times, none of these explanations seem to matter. Sometimes, your baby is just fussy at different periods. A long, fussy period in the late afternoon and evening (sometimes called the 'witching hour', around 6-8 pm) is usually called colic. Fussiness throughout the day is known as fretfulness. Tense and jumpy babies may be hypertonic.

However, fussy crying in those first few months is normal. It doesn't mean that your child is ill; your child is simply trying to adjust to the world. Your baby's nervous system isn't fully developed yet, and he'll have to adjust to all of the bodily functions like digestion that weren't necessary during gestation.

Some babies adjust to life in the world easier than others. Those who live in developing countries tend to soothe much quicker than those in industrialized countries, likely due to their closeness to their mothers during the day.

If your baby seems to be crying excessively, without any signs of being soothed in the early weeks, remember that this is not usually a problem. If you are concerned, you are always encouraged to speak to your baby's pediatrician, but remember that more often than not, this will be outgrown. Just remember that, no matter how frustrated you are, *never* shake a baby to try to stop them from fussing.

Sorting Out the Causes

Though you may eventually catch on to what your baby's various cries are, most of the time, parents catch on to the various cues instead. They also try to attempt different solutions in order to try to calm the baby down. Consider some of the following reasons that your baby may be crying:

He's hungry

Hungry babies will cry. This is most commonly the cause if it has been a while since your baby fed last, or if he didn't eat the normal amount at his previous feeding, it could be because he's hungry. If he's crying shortly after a feeding, however, he's probably not.

She wants to suck

Babies naturally crave sucking, even when not hungry. It is natural for her to crave sucking in the early months of life, and you may consider giving your baby a pacifier or her fingers.

He may have outgrown his formula or breastmilk supply

Milk supply outgrowth rarely happens overnight, but if there is a sudden decrease in volume, he may not be getting enough to eat. He could also be cluster-feeding: nursing more often to boost the supply of breastmilk. If he is rapidly polishing off bottles, then looking around as if trying to find more, he may be hungry still. You may need to feed him larger amounts of formula.

She needs to be held

Babies are designed to crave being held closely, and often. It takes being held close, wrapped up, and rocked for your baby to calm down. This recreates the sensation of being in the womb, which can help calm her down, especially when paired with white noise or the "shhh" sound.

He needs a diaper change

He may be crying because he is wet or he has recently had a bowel movement. Usually, babies don't mind being in a wet diaper unless it is irritating their skin, but a dirty diaper can be much more unpleasant.

She has indigestion

Some babies may cry because they have indigestion. She might cry for an hour or two after feeding. If this happens early on during breastfeeding, it could be caused by something Mom is eating. Cow's milk and caffeine are the two most common sensitivities of breast milk. If she drinks formula, you may need to ask a doctor to see if you should choose a different kind.

He has heartburn

He may also have heartburn. Most babies spit up to some degree, usually within their own mouths, which they swallow back down again. This can be painful if stomach acid is able to irritate the esophagus. Babies suffering from heartburn often cry after a feeding. Burping can help to alleviate the pain, but if it happens regularly, consider speaking to your baby's doctor.

She is sick

Sick babies are fussy babies. If she doesn't feel well, she's bound to be fussy. Irritability is often the first sign of illness, typically followed by a fever, vomiting, or diarrhea later. If your baby is inconsolable with signs of illness, you should call her doctor to ask about what to do next.

He is tired

If he is overtired, there's a good chance he will fussily argue about going to sleep. Some babies simply can't drift off to sleep, and they then must get over that fatigue and cry loudly before they are able to fall asleep. It happens, but it's usually outgrown.

She has something stuck to a finger or toe

If you really can't seem to find a rhyme or reason to her crying, consider checking her fingers and toes (and for boys, his penis) for hairs or threads that have wrapped around and gotten stuck. They can constrict blood flow and cause pain.

Colic

You can't treat colic if you don't know what's causing it. To treat it effectively, you must be able to figure out the cause. This is why colic in particular can be so particularly brutal for new parents: it usually has no identifiable medical cause. Rather, it comes and goes on its own, meaning there is very little that the parents can do but try to get through the crying.

But, remember Mom and Dad, this too shall pass. Your baby is not giving you a hard time: he or she is *having* a hard time. Your baby doesn't want to scream and cry; she wants you to help her

calm down. He wants you to help him to self-soothe. And of course, this will test your patience more than anything else, but I promise: it will pass. Your darling daughter or son isn't going to go off to college still crying inconsolably for two hours each evening. One day, it will stop and you'll realize that those tenuous times are over.

Most pediatricians agree that upon birth, a baby is confronted with a distressing and overwhelming experience. Nothing in utero could have prepared your sweet baby for the noise, stimulation, and sensations of life in the world. He doesn't know what's around him upon birth. He's faced with a dramatic shift and he doesn't have the coping mechanisms to figure out what's happening. Imagine that you were just picked up and dropped onto an alien planet where you don't know anyone, can't speak the language, don't understand what is good or bad, and you have to figure out how to survive. At least you, an adult, would have the coping mechanisms to reason through the situation. Your newborn child doesn't.

Instinctively, your baby may want to shut down, blocking out the overstimulation somehow. Most often, babies will sleep when they have become overstimulated simply because they can. She might not be able to walk away, but she can go to sleep. They use this as their coping mechanism. But some babies can't manage this, either. They can't self-soothe and that leaves them in a state of distress.

So, they do what babies do: they cry, often inconsolably. This is their only way of communicating, but it's also a way of further overstimulating. They make their overstimulation even worse, creating a constant cycle of inconsolable wailing. Instead of seeing the crying as something that you need to prevent as soon as possible, consider it as a form of your baby being ill-equipped to handle the world around them, so they do the only thing they can: they cry to convey that they are overwhelmed, overstimulated, and don't know what to do next.

Colicky babies are often the most alert of all. They pay attention to everything around them, quickly causing them to become overstimulated and overwhelmed. With the constant stimulation of the world around him, plus no coping mechanism to control how much he is faced with, he inevitably becomes too responsive to stimuli and cries.

Crying and Colic

It can be hard to know when your baby is crying or when your baby is colicky, especially if you've never really been around babies much in the past. All babies will cry sometimes, but when that baby continues, hour after hour, no matter what you do, there is a very good chance that it could be colic.

If no other fixes seem to help and a doctor has evaluated the baby as being healthy, the baby may simply be colicky. The definition of colic is inconsolable crying for over three hours per day, more than three days per week, and for more than three weeks.

The Two Patterns of Colic

Colic seems to follow two distinct patterns of crying. Some cry one period of time in the evening, usually between 5 and 8 pm, while being content for most of the day. During the day, the baby may be easy to console. It's tough to pinpoint what causes this form of colic.

Other babies are constantly fussy and cry all the time, day or night. They generally seem to be tense or even jumpy. They can't relax well and are quick to startle and fuss. These babies seem to respond to just about anything, such as changes in the environment, or shifting them into a new position.

Responding to Colic

When your baby is colicky, you are bound to run into frustration. There is not very much you can do to prevent colic. But, you can use five specific methods, which help soothe when nothing else seems to work.

Swaddle

In utero, babies are confined closely, tucked into their mothers' wombs without much room to flail or move around. Upon being born, they are able to move much further, which can be startling for them. By swaddling them correctly, they usually start to feel a bit more secure. This has been used for centuries to help soothe the baby.

Putting Baby on His Side or Stomach

While babies are not supposed to sleep on their stomachs, they also aren't accustomed to being placed on their backs. When they are placed on their backs, they often start into the Moro reflex; it feels as if they are falling. This is the same feeling you have when you are drifting off to sleep and then suddenly twitch yourself awake. By placing your baby on his or her side or stomach, you may be able to prevent so much crying.

However, due to an increased risk of SIDS, it is important to recognize that sleeping on the side or stomach is not safe and instead, this should only be used if you are already awake and watching your baby closely. Don't use it overnight.

White Noise

White noise machines work because they sound like the blood flow in utero. These are the shushing sounds parents make when their baby is crying or the sound created by a radio or television station that only has static. These days, there are endless apps and YouTube videos that will make these noises for you.

Movement

Movement is commonly marketed to parents, in the forms of swings, slings, jumpers, rockers, and more to help your child calm down. Intuitively, you probably already bounce and soothe your baby, gently rocking her to help her calm down. Babies spend the first nine months of their lives being rocked in utero, gently swaying as their mothers live their lives, and once they join the world, they still crave that motion.

Sucking

Sucking is naturally soothing for infants, done instinctively even before birth. Often, babies learn to suck in utero, sucking on their thumbs or fingers. It helps them to calm down. It also helps for bonding, which is why babies bond so much to their caregivers. It could take place with nursing, bottle-feeding, providing a pacifier, or letting your baby suck on his or her thumb. Letting your baby suck on something helps to encourage relaxation.

Vibration

If you've ever heard of someone driving around the block a few times to get their baby to sleep, or if you've ever placed your baby's car seat on the dryer with it running, you've managed to use vibration to help soothe your baby to sleep. Keep in mind that when using these methods, your baby should always be strapped into his or her car seat. You should also never leave your baby unattended if you are using a dryer to soothe him.

Bathing

Some babies are soothed through bathtime, but it can take some time to get both baby and parent adjusted. Many young infants may hate the bath, but using room temperature or slightly warmer water can help your baby begin to enjoy bath time and you may also get to enjoy the quiet moments.

Massages

Massages are great for relaxing babies, but you also need to be trained before doing so. It's easy to unintentionally hurt babies, so make sure that you find an infant massage class or video before beginning. Your pediatrician may have some suggestions for you.

Generally speaking, massaging in clockwise circles from the top of the limbs down is one of the most surefire ways to calm him or her down. Just make sure that you don't press too hard and avoid massaging the head and neck.

Hard-to-Calm Babies

Some babies are simply harder to calm than others. If your baby is colicky or simply fussy, you probably feel the struggles of trying to keep up with the crying. Between 10 and 20 percent of babies tend to be excessive fussers. Most are much quicker to calm down, but if yours is in that minority, you will probably feel frustrated, and that's okay! Just because she's your baby doesn't mean that her incessant crying is any easier to cope with. It's normal to feel frustrated, but remember that your baby is frustrated too. You might think that your baby is difficult, but perhaps he is just hard to calm instead of being a hard baby. He isn't trying to give you a hard time; he just doesn't know what to do.

Signs

If you are wondering if your baby is hard-to-calm, there is a good chance that yes, she probably is. Some of the most common signs include:

- You spend a lot of time trying to comfort and hold her.
- You struggle to get him to sleep more often than not.
- You call her pediatrician a lot to try to get her checked out for problems.
- You think of him as being a difficult baby or as a 'crier'.
- You feel like you've done everything you can and that nothing works.
- You are exhausted because you are coping with the crying and trying to soothe her day in and day out.

Causes

Babies all cry for different reasons, from baby to baby. This means that the reason your baby cries is likely entirely different than another baby. However, there are a few ways that you can usually identify the reason.

Hunger

Babies tend to cry during the earliest days because they're hungry. It takes a few days for breastmilk to come in when babies are born, which can lead to hunger. Babies are usually monitored closely for weight maintenance to ensure they are eating enough. If the difficulties with soothing continue beyond the first couple of months, it's probably due to other causes.

Digestive Issues

Digestive issues, such as colic, gas, or reflux usually begin in the first month and are the worst during the second. They are usually caused by either sensitivity, allergies, or temperament. Sensitivity is caused when your baby is simply easily upset by the world around them. Their only real solution is to cry. If your baby has an allergy to something in breastmilk or formula, they may have a reaction and feel sick, leading to excessive fussiness.

Temperament

Some babies are simply fussier than others as well. They may simply not be very agreeable and as a result, are easily upset. Eventually, they will learn to control this, but for now, they will be tough to manage.

Illness

Your baby may also feel sick, which can lead to crying simply because they are uncomfortable or hurting. This usually warrants a trip to a pediatrician, especially in very young children.

Getting Through the Hard Times

Though this time period is difficult to get through, one thing is true: the best thing you can do, when everything else has been done, is wait it out. Do your best to be there for your baby and trust that she will outgrow the fussiness.

It doesn't matter why your baby is crying, so much as it matters that she is. Accept that your fussy, difficult-to-calm baby will require you to spend more time with her, and embrace it. Don't let yourself get caught up in comparing her to other babies who are easier. She is her, and she is not like other babies. She is yours. And remember, it will pass. Your baby will grow, and the crying will end. For now, focus on what you can do to help soothe her.

State Control and Crying

Babies have six states of alertness, ranging from deep sleep to screaming. They may be deeply asleep, lightly asleep, drowsy, quietly alert, fussy, or screaming. The brain must learn how to control these without jumping suddenly from one to the next. Some babies are good at self-calming; they can get from fussy to back down to quiet without much help. They usually have ways to keep themselves from becoming overwhelmed. Other babies, however, don't have this support or ability to regulate their states on their own.

Babies with poor state control may find themselves struggling more often. They can't control their states. They cry and scream. They need to be swaddled and protected from overstimulation. Some of these are born prematurely or may be born addicted to drugs. They have unsteady state control, leading to them suddenly startling and shrieking, begging for help. These babies can't find a way to keep their steadiness after a day of stimulation without enough soothing. They can't keep themselves level and fall apart, screaming and crying, especially in the evening.

Cry-It-Out Questions

Most parents would do whatever they could to keep their babies from crying. They want their children to sleep at night, but also don't want to let them cry to achieve it. Unfortunately, if you want your baby to do something they don't want to do, like change a habit, that may require a bit of crying. This doesn't mean that your baby is lonely or in pain; it's a matter of teaching your baby that something else needs to happen. You probably can't keep waking up five times a night with your baby if you have work, and you probably want to enjoy a dinner without worrying about screaming. This is where teaching your baby to tolerate periods of being left alone to self-soothe comes to play.

Both you and your baby need to get enough sleep, and when neither of you is, neither of you will be happy. If Baby can't go back to sleep without you, then you will need to soothe and lull your baby, or you can teach him or her to learn to calm down instead. One of the best ways to do so is to sleep train your baby.

No, you don't need to leave your baby crying alone in a crib for long periods of time. Rather, you should place your young baby into the crib awake, but calm. See if he can sleep on his own. If he wakes up in the middle of the night, let your baby fuss a bit. If he isn't crying and screaming, let him fuss and try to self-soothe. Over time, he should be able to sleep on his own.

By about 6 months of age, your baby is ready to start coping with stress by turning to self-soothing methods. This is when your child is usually capable of sleep training. However, if both you and your partner are not on board with the process, it will not work.

To sleep train, you can start with responsiveness, gently soothing your baby when the baby is still in the crib. Only lift your baby out if the crying becomes serious. Avoid all stimulation and do not talk or fuss over the baby. Your night care must be boring and dark.

Then, set a time period that you are okay with your baby crying. It might be that you're not okay with any amount of crying, but this means that you're not likely to have much luck with sleep training. Your baby will grow to sleep through the night at some point, but it's going to be hard work up until then.

Two to three minutes is usually plenty. Let your baby fuss and cry for those three minutes. Then go in and gently reassure your baby. Repeat this every three minutes. It will be hard and your baby will likely resist any attempts to break those night feeding and waking habits, but this is the best thing you can do for her. It will be a long process that takes many days, but by the end, you and your baby will both sleep much better than you did before.

Crying after Feeding

If your baby continues to cry after feeding, you might think that your baby is crying because she's still hungry. However, if it's been less than two hours since the last feed, it's not that likely that she wants more. Instead, check other causes. Comfort her. Burp her. Bounce her gently and swaddle her. As you soothe her, she may go to sleep, or she may turn from side to side. If she does, she's looking for something to suck on. A pacifier is a good substitute if you're worried about her wanting to suck on something.

Your baby may also be crying because he is overtired. He may have been kept up for too long, leading to him feeling too fussy. He needs to rest and if your baby isn't getting enough, he may be fussier than usual. Newborns in particular are usually only awake for a handful of minutes or up to half of an hour. If your baby has been kept up later because the family wants to play pass the baby, there's a good chance that your baby's problem isn't that she's hungry; she's overstimulated!

Calming Your Baby

Even though you may not know why a baby is crying or in pain doesn't mean that you need to stop trying to soothe her. With some guesswork and some persistence, you will be able to treat those difficult babies.

Holding Him

Inconsolable babies look for being held in order to feel better. When you have a difficult-to-calm baby, try holding him more, helping him to relax and settle. You never know if he's in pain, but holding him can help to prevent it.

Upright After Feeding

Right after feeding her, make sure you keep her mostly upright for at least 20 minutes. This helps get rid of any air she may have swallowed while feeding. It also helps to dislodge any burps that may be stuck. If you place her on her back with that buildup of gas, it's possible for her to spit up or fuss the entire time, which may contribute to fussing. Holding her up helps let that gas out.

Distractions

When all else fails, you can start using distractions to help calm your baby. Try some white noise, nature sounds, or movement in order to distract your baby from their pain.

Extra Sucking Time

Sucking is a crucial way for babies to reduce pain. This is why they need a pacifier to suck on. Most babies will take to pacifiers and feel comforted by the process. A breastfed baby may also try to nurse longer in order to enjoy having something to suck on to calm down. It's less about hunger and more about wanting to have something to calm down with.

Precautions for Allergies

Allergies aren't exactly comfortable. When you have an allergy, your body is overreacting and attacking something that it shouldn't. As a result, you can be uncomfortable, in pain, or even in need of serious medical attention. If there is a family history of allergies, there's a chance that your baby may have one as well and that any inconsolable crying is directly related to it.

Take the time to remove anything that gathers dust and stop the use of chemical cleaners, using water instead, to see if it helps the baby to soothe any better.

Swaddling

Swaddling is so great for soothing hard-to-soothe babies simply because it does bring them back to a time when they were kept in the womb. Their twitching and movements can be bothersome, but by restricting the baby to just a swaddle, it's possible to help her settle down.

Keeping Yourself Calm

Having a fussy, difficult-to-calm baby can be grating for even the most patient of people. However, if you stay calm, it's easier.

Your baby picks up on your emotions and cues. Your baby will sense if you're anxious or distraught, and those feelings will be returned and mirrored. This means that keeping yourself calm is one of the most important ways to ensure that your baby will be comfortable.

Occasionally, we hear about adults who simply can't manage the sound of constant, uninterrupted crying. It's uncommon, but it does happen and the unthinkable happens in a moment. If you feel overwhelmed by the sound of your baby's crying, it's okay to stop and take a break if you need to. You aren't any less of a parent because you have to take a few minutes to nurse your own frayed nerves. Take a break if the sound is getting to you by setting your baby somewhere safe and then allow yourself to calm down for a few minutes.

What to Do In the Moment

If you feel that desperation of trying to find a way to calm your baby, you're not alone. No matter how painful it might feel for you, remember that you can control the situation. There are some simple steps you can take to try to calm down your baby and keep your own nerves from fraying.

Address Feeding Time

How are you feeding your baby? If you're nursing, can you take different positions? Is your baby gaining weight at a normal rate? How are his diapers? At 2 months of age, your baby should drink between four and six ounces of milk at each feeding. This can't be measured for breastfeeding mothers, but do you notice your baby showing hunger signs? Are diapers not fully soaked? You may want to consider measuring how much milk your body is producing by pumping before a feeding and feeding your baby through a bottle of milk.

Address Playtime

By 2 months old, your baby can stay awake for a little over an hour after feeding. During this time, your baby gets to learn all about the world. What's happening during it? Are you giving your baby alone time during this time to teach her how she can soothe herself? Have you considered having a way to unwind after playtime as you enter naptime? Especially if your baby is particularly grumpy or colicky, you might need to come up with a routine to help settle your baby and prepare for sleep.

Consider Sleep

Is your baby getting enough sleep? Make sure that you have a great sleep routine to ensure that your baby is getting the rest that he or she needs. Do you put your baby down while still awake? Do you let your baby try to self-soothe? Your baby doesn't know how to follow her own sleep cues.

You will have to help her understand when to sleep and how to make that sleep happen.

How is your baby napping? Is it catnapping in a stroller or chair or does your baby get good, long naps several times per day? If they're all less than 45 minutes, it's time to reevaluate your baby's sleep.

Consider Your Baby

You should also take a good look, physically and metaphorically, at your baby. How long does your baby cry each day? Is there an obvious sign of discomfort, such as eczema or GERD? Is your baby simply a difficult-to-soothe temperament? How long do you hold him? Some babies yearn for that physical touch. Remember, closeness is one of the Three C's of Contentment, after all.

Consider Your Own Role

What did you expect to get out of motherhood? Did you assume that your baby would be their own person that you wouldn't have to do much with? Are your expectations being unmet because they are unreasonable compared to what they could be? Are you having a hard time taking your baby's temperament in stride because it doesn't align with what kind of baby you thought you'd have?

You can't plan what kind of child you will have; that is entirely based on temperament. While no one likes tears, some babies cry more or less. Make sure that your attitude is reasonable and remind yourself that you couldn't have planned for temperament. Though you can't control temperament, you can control a routine to ensure that your baby's emotions are regulated.

Routine, Self-Soothing, and Setting Your Baby and You up for Success

Dealing with a difficult-to-soothe baby can be nerve-wracking, but you can set yourself and your baby up for success with a few simple changes to your parenting routine. From being able to recognize that your baby's needs must be balanced with your own, you can start making it easier to prevent anyone's nerves from fraying. You just have to know what you're doing.

Comfort Within Reason

You may feel sorry for your baby as she cries. Yes, she needs to be held and comforted, but you have to recognize that your baby needs to have other opportunities to learn to self-soothe. If you simply take over for your baby every time that he or she is feeling upset, how is she going to learn how to soothe later on?

Babies become accustomed to being soothed by you as you hold them, and then that is their only method of soothing. That's not good for anyone when you want to sleep and your baby doesn't know what to do. A little fussing is okay. You don't have to leave your baby to cry it out in the sense that they cry until they stop; you just have to give your baby the space needed to grow and learn.

Let Your Baby Soothe Himself

Your baby needs the opportunity to practice soothing. You may still need to hold your baby sometimes, and that's okay too. But, you aren't always available to meet your baby's every beck and call. Will she be going to daycare? Will you be able to always drop everything to go tend to her needs? Will you be able to wake up every time something startles your baby awake, or do you need your baby to find a way to soothe on her own?

Most parents will, at some point, need to teach their baby to self-soothe. Whether that comes earlier or later will be up to you, but it's often easier before you set the expectation that the only method for soothing is in the arms of Baby's parents. When it's bedtime, swaddle up your baby and as soon as she's calm, put her in the crib. She'll get the idea after enough time and the predictability of knowing that she is about to be put down will help her to adjust.

Treat Your Own Exhaustion

If you are burning the candle on both ends, you probably don't have the mental energy to deal with creating a routine or some other way to keep your baby soothed and calm. It's okay to be frustrated and exhausted, especially if you're spending your day with constantly crying babies. However, you need to take care of yourself, too. If you want to treat your own exhaustion, the best starting point is to get a good sleep routine for your baby. The more you adjust your baby's routine, the better you'll feel.

So, how do you do this? Simple: you sleep. You get your baby to sleep well. Get Baby ready to sleep before the fussiness begins, at the first signs of sleepiness to avoid the meltdown of being overstimulated. The most basic routine to implement this? Feed your baby, play with your baby, change your baby's diaper, swaddle, cuddle, then place the baby in the crib to sleep. It's really that simple: feed, play, sleep.

With this routine, while giving your baby enough space to grow more comfortable with her fussiness and self-soothing, you should have a happy baby. Happy parents make for happy babies and by meeting all of your baby's cues before they get to pressing needs, your baby will be happier and healthier.

CHAPTER 3 - SLEEP SCHEDULES ARE KEY TO SUCCESS

When babies sleep, they are among the calmest, most beautiful sights one can see. There's not much like watching your baby sleeping peacefully and contentedly. That contented, peaceful sleep, however, isn't generated easily. You have to work for it. You will have to ensure that you calm your baby down and prepare them to start sleeping well. Your child's sleep cycles vary greatly, especially compared to your own as an adult, but that's okay! You and your baby have greatly different needs right now. Your baby needs to sleep to learn and grow. You need sleep to refresh your body.

Sleep is an essential function that is necessary for that recharge. It helps you to sort through memories and consolidate the ones that will go into long-term storage. It can help you to think clearly and process your memories as well. Your baby's sleep needs are much, much higher than those of an adult simply because your baby is doing a lot more learning and growing than any adult. Did you know that by the time that your baby is just 5 years of age, their brain is already 90% of the size it will be as an adult? There is a lot of learning going on in those days and your baby sleeps to help create those memories.

This means that sleep becomes one of the most essential needs that you must meet for your baby. You must be able to help your child soothe into a peaceful sleep to help him or her get enough of it. Of course, babies don't always want to cooperate. You may get the dreaded witching hour, or the dreaded sleep regressions coming along, destroying any semblance of a routine that you already had. It can be extremely frustrating to see all of your progress disappear, but it's not gone forever.

As you read through this chapter, we're going to go over the ins and outs of sleep for your baby. You will learn all about helping your baby to soothe him or herself to sleep and enjoy the peaceful moments, where hopefully, you can get in a bit of shut-eye too.

Children's Sleep Cycles

Children's sleep cycles vary greatly compared to those of adults. Without the sleep they need, your child is more likely to feel groggy and heavy. They're more likely to feel grumpy and be irritable when something happens. Setting your baby up for emotional success is often as easy as learning your little one's sleepy cues and meeting them before your baby can work herself up into a tizzy.

Adults need between 7 and 9 hours of sleep per day, with sleep cycles of every 90 minutes, and typically get the bulk of their sleep in one uninterrupted block. In your baby, however, that sleep cycle is much shorter: it's just 60 minutes instead, and your baby has to wake up several times in order to meet needs. Your newborn's stomach isn't big enough to let him sleep overnight yet; he needs the nourishment to fuel his growth!

That shorter sleep cycle means more irritability in a lot of cases, however. Once that cycle loops through, your baby will be more prone to waking, which can be a problem if your baby doesn't learn how to soothe back to sleep.

Your baby will need different amounts of sleep, depending on how old he or she is. These sleep needs change rapidly, so you must be able to adjust and accommodate the ever-changing demands your sweet little one has.

See the table below for guidelines on how much you can expect your baby to sleep.

Age	Sleep Requirement
Newborn - 3 months	14 to 17 hours of sleep per 24 hours; spurts of 2 to 4 hours with 2 to 5 daytime naps and the rest of sleep at night.
4 - 6 months	12 to 16 hours per 24 hours; sleeping through the night (5 hours of sleep or more) happens at this age. Your baby will take 3 naps daily.
7 - 11 months	12 to 16 hours per 24 hours; sleep is 10 to 12 hours at night with two daytime naps.
12 - 17 months	11 to 14 hours, with 1 to 2 naps.
18 months +	11 to 14 hours, with one long daytime nap.

As discussed, babies tend to be fussiest toward the end of their wake cycles. They start to feel overwhelmed and frustrated with their surroundings. This makes sense when we go back to the idea of state control. Your baby can't control her emotions as much at that point; she uses sleep to regulate her own stimulation and drifts off to sort of get a mental reset. You need to make sure that your baby gets to sleep regularly and within normal time frames for her own wellbeing.

Choosing the Right Bedding

If you're designing your baby's sleep space, you're probably wondering about blankets. Generally, blankets are no longer recommended for young babies when sleeping alone in a crib, as they are too easy for Baby to accidentally cover her face with. If you must use a blanket, it's usually better to use a wearable blanket or a "Sleep Sack" in order to keep your baby covered up without

the risk of covering up her face as well. You may also choose to use a fleece sleeper instead of a blanket, which should be plenty warm enough in a normally room-temperature bedroom.

When choosing blankets, it's usually recommended to choose acrylic or polyester cotton, as these are easily washed and non-allergenic. The catch is, you must make sure that there aren't any holes, long threads, or fringe decorations that may get stuck on fingers or toes. You also don't want the blanket to be large enough that your baby could get caught in it.

If you have a young baby, cotton receiving blankets are great for wrapping around a baby that would likely kick off their coverings. Your baby's bed should also have a plastic mattress cover. Let's be real; babies are *messy*. Unless you want a bed that has had a chance to absorb all of the potential bodily fluids that your baby could leave behind, you want to keep the mattress sufficiently protected with a mattress cover. A cloth mattress pad will allow for the air to circulate under the sheet. Then, the sheet goes right over the mattress pad. You will want between 3 and 6 sheets and mattress covers. After all, you don't want to run out overnight if your baby happens to have a few accidents.

Positioning Your Baby to Avoid SIDS

Sudden Infant Death Syndrome (SIDS) is something that every new parent worries about. Sometimes known as crib death, this is when a baby, 12 months or younger, passes away during sleep without any clear reason or warning signs. There are no ways to completely eliminate the risk, but you can reduce it. The American Academy of Pediatrics, in 1992, recommended that babies be put to sleep on their backs, and since their 1994 Back to Sleep campaign, there has been a dramatic drop in SIDS rates. In comparison, in 1992, the SIDS death rate was 103 per 100,000 births, and by 2018, had been reduced down to just 35.

The best position to avoid SIDS is to always put your baby to sleep on their back. When you put your baby in bed on her back, you help to prevent her from pushing her face in the mattress, which could smother her. Putting your baby on her side, while effective in calming colic, is also risky as your baby could roll onto her stomach without you knowing, which could be dangerous.

It's not worth trying even once, as the potential loss is unimaginable. If you worry about your baby sleeping on her back and choking on spit-up, try not to worry so much; most babies are able to swallow or cough up those fluids automatically.

Prepare for a Good Sleep for Your Baby: Birth to 3 Months

Routines are essential to any baby's wellbeing. Any time I hear someone telling me that their young baby isn't eating or sleeping well, I always ask questions about their routines. And most of the time, they don't have one! They always tell me, "Well, why would I need a routine? Won't my baby just eat and play and sleep on her own time anyway?" Well, yes, to an extent. But, routines are flexible. You can start a routine that will guide you and your baby. As a result, you'll have a happier baby.

Remember consistency? That's where a routine comes in! Now, you might think that you can't be consistent while still responding to cues, but that's where you're wrong. If your baby is truly tired an hour before you'd normally have naptime, there's probably a good reason for it. It's best for everyone if you do put your baby to sleep. But, by and large, your child's schedule and natural rhythm will be relatively predictable. You should be able to tell when your baby is hungry based on the time. Don't believe me? Spend a week recording down when your baby eats and sleeps. You'll probably realize pretty quickly that everything is at pretty consistent times!

Routines bring order to the world and teach your baby that all needs will always be met. It strengthens the bond between parent and child, and your baby will become happier and easier to take care of because she knows what to expect. This also means that when you need to leave your baby with a babysitter (or grandma!), you can know what they need to make the process go as smoothly as possible.

Putting Baby in Their Own Bed

Generally, it's a good idea for babies to sleep in their own beds. Most recommendations agree that to prevent SIDS, most babies are safest on their own. However, they should still co-sleep, meaning they should be in your bedroom. By co-sleeping, you actually *reduce* the risk of SIDS. However, you must also have your baby in your room during that time.

Bedsharing in the "family bed", as it's called, can be done safely, but only if very stringent safety measures are taken, and not following those safety requirements can be devastating, so I prefer to recommend that babies sleep on their own.

If you do choose to bed share, keep in mind that in order to do it safely, the mother must be breastfeeding, neither parent can smoke, the bed must be stripped down to avoid suffocation, and any potential cracks or crevasses that the baby could fall into must be covered up. It's also not safe if either parent is on medication, drinking, or is on less than four hours of sleep at any given point in time.

Good Sleep Routines

Good sleep routines require you to understand what your routine needs as well as what the steps are to getting your baby to fall asleep.

The Keys to a Good Sleep Routine

A good sleep routine has four key components. You must provide time for eating, time for play, time for care, and time for sleep. These four components are necessary to ensure that your baby's needs are all met, leading to a gentle transition to a sleeping baby.

Nutrition

First, you must provide food. This sounds like common sense, but it should also be the first point in your routine. When your baby wakes up, he's probably hungry. And, by feeding him when he first wakes up, you ensure that he'll have a more even mood, making him easier to play with.

Play

Your baby also needs time to play and explore. This helps to bond you with your child. Even the time that you spend rocking, holding, and tickling your baby is a way of playing. Talking and engaging with your baby is a way that you can play and bond, and your baby will learn more and more about the world in doing so.

Talk to your child about what you're doing. Tell your child about your day or routine. This time is crucial to stimulate her brain and body. There won't be as much of this time at first but over time, you will get more of it. You might be tempted to go out and buy all sorts of new baby toys. They can be adorable, but it's still a little early. Our baby doesn't need fancy toys or gadgets to keep him busy; he wants you!

Care

Third, your baby needs time for care. This includes a lot of activities like diaper changes, bathing, grooming, and the like. This time is spent making sure that your child's other needs are met while still providing him with that crucial interaction.

Sleep

Finally, your baby needs sleep. More specifically, she needs to learn how to sleep on her own without you shushing, nursing, or rocking her to sleep. You need to give her the foundation she needs to live her life her way, and that comes from teaching your baby to sleep the right way. Putting her down drowsy, but awake and calm, is the best way to encourage her to fall asleep.

Your Caffeine and Your Baby

In those early days, it's so easy to feel like you need coffee. You're running on broken sleep, have a lot to do, and probably turn straight to caffeine for that additional boost of energy. But, what you eat and drink can impact your baby. Coffee, in particular, can enter breast milk. Especially if you drink more than one or two cups of coffee daily as a breastfeeding mother. You may keep your baby awake longer, causing fussiness and grumpiness. Keep the caffeine to a minimum and focus on eating well and sleeping when you can to keep your energy levels up.

Good vs Bad Sleep Cues

Your baby will give you specific sleep cues that can help you to tell that he or she is sleepy.

Paying attention to these will help you know when your baby should go to sleep.

Creating the Right Environment

If you want to create an environment that your child will be able to sleep well, you can do so with seven key rules. These steps will help you to create the right routine that will gently lull your child to sleep and teach him to sleep on his own.

1. Move away from the busy part of the household. Try to find somewhere without television, chatting, or stimulation.
2. Bathe, massage, and dress your baby in pajamas.
3. Darken the room with blackout curtains.
4. Feed, burp, and change your baby. This should be about an hour later now.
5. Swaddle your baby.

6. Hold your baby in an upright position for 10 to 20 minutes after feeding.

7. Place the baby in the crib, drowsy but awake. Use a sleep aid, like white noise. Then give him the chance to fall asleep on his own. Let him fuss a little bit and don't pick him up unless he's really crying and unable to calm himself down.

Providing Sleep Aids

Babies do need some help to fall asleep. They need to be able to calm down, which can be done with a cuddle, bath, massage, or a dark room. However, you may want to provide your baby with a bit of extra sleep help. Some babies will be perfectly fine sleeping on their own, but some need some help. Think about how many young children need to have their favorite plushie or blanket to fall asleep. Your baby may need something as well.

Pacifiers

Babies naturally try to suck when they are upset, overstimulated, or hurt. This is because sucking helps to produce endorphins, the feel-good hormones in the brain. Over time, the need to suck starts to fade, but others may need to have an alternative option given to them, and a pacifier is preferred to Mom's breast, simply because Mom won't always be around. The pacifier is also a tool that your baby will be able to rely on overnight as well, especially as he or she gets older and can pick it up on her own around 5 months old.

Be careful about introducing pacifiers. They should be added only after Baby is adjusted to breastfeeding to prevent nipple confusion. You also don't want to rely on pacifiers heavily. Don't give it until Baby has established that she needs it, such as if she's fussy or crying when you're trying to put her to sleep.

Comfort Items

At just 1 month old, your baby can't choose a security object yet. Stuffed animals or blankets aren't going to be comforting yet. But, you can introduce the idea now and allow your child to adapt to it. Your child can get used to having the item nearby, and soon, will associate that item with comfort.

Music and Other Sounds

We sing to babies to calm them down. We shush them to help soothe them to comfort. But we can't always do this. It's easy to include a white noise machine or a small speaker that plays a soft playlist in your baby's nursery. As a bonus, this also helps to drown out normal day-to-day sounds that could otherwise wake up your baby.

Visual Stimulation

You want your baby to love being in her crib, so you want to provide some things that also keep her happy. Adding things to look at is perfect. Babies prefer to look specifically at the faces of people, but they may also enjoy looking at images with strong contrast. Your baby's vision is still quite fuzzy in the early days and months, so the strong contrast allows them to really see the difference between objects. Mobiles, pictures, and other attractive things can be a great way to add visual interest to your nursery.

The Wrong Sleep Cues

It's easy to unintentionally teach your baby the wrong lesson about sleep by setting expectations that you do not care to keep long-term. Yes, it's nice to cuddle a baby to sleep in your arms, but in doing so, you're teaching her that she should sleep in arms. She likes it, too! It's comfortable and enjoyable. But this isn't good for either of you long term.

Wait After Feeding for Sleep!

You don't want your baby to go to sleep right after a feeding. This makes feeding the sleep cue and you may not be able to get him to sleep again in the middle of the night without feeding your baby, even when he no longer needs the middle of the night calories.

Don't Let Him Play in Bed

It's tempting to leave your baby in the crib when you need to do something, but you should keep the crib specific to sleeping. This means not letting your baby play in your bed. Use a playpen or a tummy time mat instead to create that differentiation.

Don't be Her Only Source of Soothing

Yes, it's natural for you to reach for your baby at every fuss. But you're not helping either of you. A bit of fussing will help your baby learn to settle on her own.

The Fourth Trimester

When taking care of your baby, one of the best things that you can do is consider the first three months of your baby's life as an extension of pregnancy. Human babies are born before they're really fully developed and ready to live on their own, even compared to many other species. They are incredibly fragile, can't hold their heads up, and can barely control their own movements due to their immature nervous system.

Ideally, babies would have an additional few months in the womb, but the human body is simply not built to accommodate this. Our hips are too narrow to allow for the passage of a baby that has gestated as long as expected for animals our size. They should need an additional three months in the womb, which is where the idea of the fourth trimester comes.

During the fourth trimester, babies crave closeness, cuddling, and need their needs met quickly.

And, to meet those needs, imagine yourself as the womb.

The Five S's of Calming

Babies cry to communicate, but sometimes, it might feel like it's hard to know what they're doing or what they need. By mimicking the womb, you can help calm your baby down using the Five S's of Calming.

Swaddling

Swaddling works to recreate the snugness of the womb. Wrapped-up babies feel like they're contained the same way they were in the womb. This helps them to stay calm and quiet.

Side/Stomach

The back is the best place to sleep, but when it comes to calmness, the side is the best. Hold your baby on the side.

Shushing

In the womb, babies hear the sound of blood flow, which is actually louder than a vacuum! This sound is constantly playing around them and the silence of the world can be startling to babies. Shushing sounds, with a rumbling to it, will help to calm your baby before you know it.

Swinging

Living in the womb involves constant shaking and swaying. Just like the ice that bobs around in your cup as you go up a flight of stairs, your baby is jostled around as well. Slow rocking may keep a baby calm and content, but most crying babies respond better to quicker swaying. Note that you shouldn't shake your baby; swaying while carefully supporting your baby's head is best.

Sucking

Finally, the last of the five is sucking. Your baby will be relaxed quickly with something to suck on, whether that's a bottle, a breast, or a pacifier.

Sleep at 6 Months

By 6 months old, your baby may be a good napper, but others may not be. A consistent routine is key to ensuring your baby gets enough sleep, especially because the day is full of exciting activities. Your baby should have two naps in the daytime, usually a shorter morning nap, plus a

longer one after lunch. Sleep may be worsened by teething, especially if naps are too short and under 45 minutes at a time throughout the day. Try to condense naps down with good scheduling.

Sleep at 8 Months

Around 8 months of age, your baby is staying awake for longer periods of time. Most need around 14 hours during a 24-hour period. This is typically between 9 and 12 hours at night and 3 to 4 during the day, usually in a morning and afternoon nap.

However, at this age, there is a big sleep regression; a period when your baby's mind is developing rapidly and she's trying to develop a new major milestone. You may have a few days or weeks of your baby struggling to sleep. Don't worry! Stick to the routine and the hard times will pass before you know it.

Controlling Your Child's Circadian Rhythm

Adult sleep is ruled by a circadian rhythm; a pattern of physiological changes that cycle through 24 hours at a time based on light exposure. Your body's internal clock knows that when the sun is up, you should be up as well. Darkness, on the other hand, tells your body to go to sleep.

Newborns, however, are not governed by these rhythms. In the womb, your baby's schedule was dictated by his mother's body. He would be calmer when his mother was sleeping and he would be active and awake when his mother was awake. After birth, this was severed and he had to start making his own rhythm instead.

Your baby will take 12 weeks, or possibly longer, in order to show the day-night rhythm of melatonin, and it will take longer for cortisol to develop. It may take up to 5 months for your baby to have a reliable cycle. To help your baby develop that cycle sooner, consider the following:

1. Make your baby part of the daily routine. By including

your baby in your daily activities, you can help trigger the day-night cycle.

2. Reduce nighttime stimulation. By keeping nighttime stimulation to a minimum, your baby is going to get more rest at night.

3. Use natural lighting patterns. Let your baby be exposed to the afternoon sunlight, and make sure nighttime is dark. Babies who spend plenty of time outdoors may develop stronger circadian rhythms.

CHAPTER 4 - SUCCESSFUL FEEDING ROUTINES MAKE HAPPY BABIES

Feeding your baby is a major responsibility. You will likely spend a lot of your time attempting to get him or her to eat something. Whether you have a newborn or a baby who has begun to enjoy eating solid foods, your baby will need you to provide them with healthy, nutritious options that will keep him well nourished.

In this chapter, we'll address some of the most vital topics, including choosing between breast or formula, solving common feeding problems, teaching your child to eat well, and weaning your baby onto solids.

Breast or Formula?

One of the biggest decisions that parents must make is to decide whether they will feed their baby through breastfeeding or formula. Now, on a technicality, breastmilk *is* the best for your baby. Your baby's milk will be tailored specifically to his or her needs as Mom nurses. However, if you can't breastfeed for any reason (including if you just can't handle the stress of it!), feeding with formula is still a valid decision.

Breastmilk is what is created specifically to raise young human babies; it's good for health, brain development, and bonding, but if you can't make breastfeeding work, that's completely fine. Don't let a fear of failure make you doubt yourself or your own maternal instincts. Many women choose to breastfeed part-time with their babies when they can. Others skip it entirely. The decisions that you make will be up to you. If you choose to formula feed or you cannot breastfeed, your baby will still be just fine.

Special Considerations for the Breastfeeding Mother

Before you breastfeed your baby, there are a few key considerations that you need to make. Feeding matters, and if you aren't careful, something that you thought may be beneficial could actually be incompatible with breastfeeding in general. If you're nursing your baby, keep in mind the following things to avoid:

- **Don't Exercise Before Feeding:** This may cause lactic acid to build up in the milk after exercising.
- **Avoid Eating Different Foods:** When you start eating new foods with strong flavors, you may cause your baby to avoid your milk. The foods you eat flavor your milk and begin shaping your baby's palate.

- **Avoid Medications that can Enter Breast Milk:** Certain medications are not fit for breastfeeding. Your doctor will be able to tell you more about whether the foods you're consuming are fit for breastfeeding or not. Not all medication passes through breast milk. Some medication may also prevent you from developing milk at all.

- **Avoid Lotions on the Breast:** Any lotion on the breast can cause your baby to turn away due to the taste. It also isn't a good idea for your baby to be eating lotion in the first place. If your breasts or nipples are chapped, consider lanolin cream.

- **Avoid Stress:** Stress can, in some cases, cripple your milk supply. If it doesn't, it may cause your milk to taste different as well.

The First Week

During the first week of your baby's life, you will be faced with a wide range of lifestyle changes, the likes of which you probably never fully expected. Nutrition is critical at this age for your baby, which can put a lot of stress on any parent. If you (or your partner) are breastfeeding, this time is filled with trying to discover how to nurse the baby while also adjusting to all of the physical changes that come along with childbirth. It can take 2 to 5 days for milk to begin to flow.

Before that point, your baby will be getting calorie and nutrient-dense colostrum, the "liquid gold" of breast milk. Generally, during the first couple of days, the colostrum is enough for your baby, especially if your baby is not showing hunger cues. However, if your baby does appear to be hungry, even with the colostrum, you may need to "top up" or supplement with formula.

During this first week, as stressed as you may be, remember that the mother's relaxation is key to developing and producing milk. If you are too stressed out, milk production can slow, or even stall in certain cases. Try to relax during this time. Unless something seems off, your baby is probably fine.

How Often Do I Feed My Baby?

Your baby should be fed "on demand". This means that when your baby shows hunger cues, you should feed her. Or, if she has slept longer than three hours, she needs to nurse as well. The early days are draining; sucking to draw the milk and colostrum takes a lot of energy for a tiny newborn, and he will need the practice and strength to do so. Nursing on demand also allows your milk supply to be established and stimulated. Your body will produce milk to the demand placed by your baby.

Whether feeding formula or breastmilk, your baby will eat between eight and twelve times during any 24-hour period, with the exception being a cluster-feeding newborn trying to build up your milk supply. At this stage, there's no need to schedule feedings; just provide your baby with food as needed, following his cues. Respond to your baby's cues as needed.

How Long Should a Feeding Last?

A feeding usually isn't that long in the early days. Bottle-fed babies may finish their bottle in 15 or 20 minutes. Breastfed babies may take much longer; he could take 20 to 40 minutes, especially in the early days. Baby bottles tend to let more liquid through and take less work to drink than breastfeeding.

How Do I Know if My Baby is Getting Enough to Eat?

It's easy to track how much you're feeding your baby if you have formula; you simply measure the amounts consumed in bottles each day. Start with a three-ounce bottle and let your baby drink it to see how much she consumes. Keep in mind that her stomach is tiny in those early days and she probably won't be able to drink much more than one or two ounces. Eventually, she will be drinking between 18 and 20 ounces per 24-hour period. Keep this guideline in mind and follow your baby's cues. She'll let you know what you need.

When you breastfeed, there's a lot more guesswork. Typically, breastfeeding for 20 to 40 minutes is enough. However, milk production isn't always consistent throughout the day, and depending on the baby, they may get less if they are not nursing efficiently. You will have to go solely on your baby's cues to determine if he's getting enough breastmilk.

How Often Do I Have to Burp My Baby?

Babies will ingest air as they suck down their formula. This means that you will need to burp your baby to make sure that they can clear out the air trapped in their little tummies. By doing this, you can usually cut out the risk of spitting up the milk or formula they have consumed. Burping should happen regularly, but you'll need to know the cues to see if your baby needs a good burp or not.

If you don't get a cue from a formula-fed baby, you may want to break 10 to 15 minutes into feeding to burp him before allowing him to finish the bottle, or to finish feeding, until he is done. Breastfed babies, on the other hand, should be burped upon finishing up their feeding.

Some babies will burp easily with a quick pat on the back. Look for your baby to stop feeding and squirm or fuss–he may need to burp. If he starts moving around after setting him down after the feeding, he also probably needs to burp.

Do I Have to Take Special Precautions with Baby Bottles?

If you are bottle-feeding your baby at all, it's important to consider some special precautions. Your baby's immune system is immature at this age, so you must make sure that you clean the bottle before feeding your baby. If you live somewhere with contaminated water, you may want to boil or buy clean water for formula. The nipple and bottle should be sterilized for the first use, and after that, they can be washed in the dishwasher or hand washed.

Just as you'd take precautions for your own food handling, you should take similar ones for your baby. Wash your hands before handling formula or bottles. Then, wash the bottles immediately after finishing a feeding to prevent milk residue from building up.

Burping Tips

If your baby is squirming, fussing, and showing all the signs of being uncomfortable during or after a feeding, he probably needs to burp. However, not all burps will come easily or naturally for the baby. Sometimes, you have to be a bit creative with the poses you take to help your baby get the burp out. If your baby doesn't burp within a minute or two in one pose, move to the next. You need to help him burp after each feeding.

The easiest burping pose involves holding your baby up, letting his head rest on your shoulder. Use one hand to support the baby's head and back while the other pats at his back gently to help loosen any gas bubbles.

If that doesn't work, sit your baby up on your lap, letting his chest and head rest in one hand while cradling his chin in the palm of your hand and the heel on his chest. Gently pat your baby's back with your other hand until he burps.

If that doesn't work, you could try placing your baby face-down on your lap, supporting his head so it is higher than his chest, and rub and pat his back gently. You don't want him to spit up–you just want the gas to be relieved!

What to Do When Baby Falls Asleep While Eating

In the earliest days, eating is hard work! It's tough to be able to suck in all that food. Sometimes, they may sleep through a feeding entirely. Whether your baby falls asleep ten minutes into eating or is sleeping through feedings, in those newborn days, you need to wake them up. Your newborn spent all of her gestation being provided all of her needs through the umbilical cord. Now, you have to sustain her with milk.

We've already talked about how overwhelmed babies sleep more because they are trying to block out stimulation. You will see this happening with your baby. In the first few days, your baby is likely to sleep more simply because she's overwhelmed with suddenly needing to breathe on her own, eat on her own, and feel the sensations of the world.

They may also be swaddled during the feeding, which can encourage her to fall asleep as well.

If swaddled, your baby will be nice and cozy and is much more likely to fall asleep.

Another reason for not drinking as much as necessary is not getting enough nutrition. It might sound counterintuitive, but without enough nutrition, she can't muster up the energy to keep up with the feeding. This could happen due to a missed feeding, dwindling milk supply, or being given water. Water is unnecessary at this age and takes up space that could have been used for milk or formula.

Generally, a breastfed baby who sleeps longer than three hours, or a formula-fed baby who sleeps longer than three and a half hours, must be woken up to eat. If she is falling asleep in the middle of the feeding, gently wake her up. Tickle her feet or blow on her face. She needs to stay awake to get that precious nutrition! If you fail to do this, you may wind up with a snacker: a baby who wants to feed a small amount every hour, day and night. This could be a major problem later on when trying to correct sleep habits.

Some common ways to keep your baby awake include burping him upright, changing his diaper halfway through the feeding, feeding the baby without clothes on and without a blanket to prevent him from being warm and cozy, or even using a damp rag with tepid water to gently tickle his face to wake him up.

The Fourth and Fifth Months

By months four and five, your baby will be able to consume more milk. This means that feedings will stretch out to closer to three or four hours apart. You may also notice your baby dropping their nighttime feeding around this time (or they might not). This is acceptable as long as they weigh at least 14 pounds before dropping that feeding and they consume five to six 6-ounce bottles each day. Your baby, at this age, needs roughly 30 ounces of formula each 24-hour period.

Breastfed babies will eat about the same, though it is difficult to measure unless you are pumping and bottle-feeding. At this age, babies are preparing to start eating solid foods as well. Typically, eating solids begins around 6 months of age, though it may, in some cases, happen earlier.

Feeding at 6 Months

At 6 months of age, your baby is ready to begin solids. It's an exciting time, fraught with both joy at watching your baby take one more step toward becoming a self-sufficient little person and fear that you might mess it up. Choking may be a major concern, or you may worry about allergies or some other situation that could become dangerous.

Introducing foods is easy. The hard part is keeping it all contained without a big mess, but messes are just part of life! And who can resist laughing and snapping a picture of a baby who dunked their whole face in their dinner?

Too Much or Too Little?

Adding solids to your child's diet may be intimidating if you're unsure he's eating enough. However, if you remember that you never have a reason to force-feed a healthy baby, it gets easier. Your baby can self-regulate. By offering, but never forcing, your baby to eat, you allow your baby to work out how much he or she needs to eat at any given time on their own. Your baby should be allowed to follow their own digestive cues. Provide the food. What your baby does with it after you provide it is up to her.

Whether you have a history of allergies in your family or not, it's a good idea to introduce new foods carefully and strategically to ensure that your baby isn't allergic to anything. Consider following these steps to introduce new foods.

1. Begin with solid foods and new liquids. Some may buy prepared foods while others may make their own purees for their babies. Others still may choose to use what is called "baby-led weaning". This is a process in which the baby is provided with soft foods that can be gummed without risking choking, such as bananas, a steamed potato cut into pieces a child can grasp, and other similar soft foods.

2. Continue feeding milk or formula. No matter how much you offer solid foods, your baby still gets most nutritional needs met through breastmilk or formula.

3. Give water to drink with solid foods. Juices are high in sugars and are better off avoided until later. Let your child enjoy real fruit instead.

4. Have feeding time in a high chair, adjusted to your baby's ability to sit upright. Use a bib to minimize mess, or keep your baby shirtless and plan on a quick

rinse in the shower after mealtime. You may consider giving her a spoon as well to play with to entice her to keep her mouth open.

5. Introduce cereals with breast milk or formula first, then move on to lightly colored fruits and veggies. You could begin with a banana smashed into her cereal, or an apple or pear puree. Then, introduce vegetables after.

6. Make sure that you introduce only one new food every three to four days to make sure you can look out for allergic reactions. Pay close attention to signs of mood changes or discomfort. Eventually, your baby will be ready to start eating solid foods a few times per day.

Introducing Harder to Digest Food

Some foods are simply harder for the body to digest, or they are more likely to trigger an allergic reaction. Consider holding off certain foods to the following ages:

Age	Food
7 months	Egg yolks
8 months	Meats
9 months	Soy, beans, cheese, yogurt
12 months	Cow's milk, egg whites, fish, chocolate, citrus, chestnuts, tomatoes, strawberries, honey

Night Feeding at 7 Months Old

By 7 months of age, your baby no longer requires night feeding. Your baby should be getting plenty of nutrition during the day. If your baby still wakes up at night at 7 months old, it may be time for sleep training. At this point, it is habit waking your baby up each night. You can train your baby to sleep through the night at this stage pretty easily, if you can tolerate a bit of crying.

Start with a basic sleep ritual. It should be the same every single night: feed the baby, bathe and massage your baby, make the room dark, and place your baby in the crib while still awake. If your baby accepts this, great! If not, you may need to keep working with him.

When you know that your baby is neither hungry nor in pain, you can start teaching him to break the crying cycle. Let him cry for three minutes, so long as he is not hysterical. Keep in mind that your baby is crying because he wants you to hold or feed him. After all, that is routine (remember the importance of consistency?). Now, it's time to create a new routine: one in which everyone gets to enjoy more sleep. If the cry is frantic and you can't tell if something is wrong, check on him.

This teaches your baby that your baby has to soothe himself. If he doesn't desperately need something, he should be okay to soothe himself if you set him up with the right tools. When you do enter the room, keep it quiet and uninteresting. You can pat his back and give him his pacifier, then leave the room.

Complete this over and over, soothing without holding the baby. Only pick him up if he is screaming and bawling. A bit of fussing is okay. Hysterical screaming is not. But, remember not to hold him until he falls asleep–put him down drowsy, but awake. Complete this process until your baby falls asleep.

Finger Foods

By the age of 8 months old, your baby is old enough to start enjoying bite-sized finger foods.

This is a great step toward feeding himself. If it can dissolve in the mouth, it is good finger food.

There are many puffs and cereal crisps that meet this standard. For now, feeding will be with the hands, but it doesn't hurt to give him a spoon or fork to play with at the same time.

Common Baby Feeding Myths

When you're a new parent, you probably get information from dozens of sources. People at the grocery store may comment unprompted about something. You might have old-fashioned family members pushing their own parenting methods, even though some of them may be quite outdated. You will probably start to hear all sorts of myths surrounding your baby, and the topic of feeding babies seems to have all sorts of parents on different pages.

Baby is Allergic to Mom's Milk

Some people falsely believe that babies are allergic to their mother's milk. However, this is false: babies are designed to drink milk from their mothers. However, babies may be allergic to parts of Mom's diet, which enters the milk after she consumes it.

Breastfed Babies Need Water

Especially in hotter climates, you will probably hear that your baby needs water. This is untrue; breastfed infants only need breast milk until they are older. Unless your doctor recommends providing water to a breastfed baby for other reasons, it is unnecessary until your baby begins eating solid foods.

You Can't Get Pregnant While Breastfeeding

Contrary to popular belief, breastfeeding is not a reliable source of birth control. While some women may not have their periods for months, or even until weaning, this is not the case for everyone. It may make it improbable for ovulation to occur, especially when exclusively breastfeeding (meaning no solids or water), but it is still possible. If you don't want to have another baby, don't use breastfeeding as a form of birth control.

Signs Baby Isn't Getting Enough Nutrition

You probably worry about whether your baby is getting enough nutrition, and this is a common enough worry. This is especially the case with breastfeeding since you can't regulate and see how much your baby is eating. Some formula-fed babies may also suffer from signs that they aren't getting enough nutrition as well. Your doctor will catch this through weight checks. In particular, babies must have regained the 10% of birth weight lost at the two-week mark. If this is not the case, the baby may not be eating enough. The most common signs include:

- **Feedings take 10 minutes or less:** Your baby needs to eat often, but by the second week, your baby should be able to consume more food in less time, but usually, 20 minutes is the golden rule for breastfeeding and 15 minutes is quick for bottle-fed infants. If they are eating less than that, there may be a problem.

- **Baby fusses while feeding:** A fussy baby probably needs to burp during feeding. However, it can also be a sign your baby isn't getting enough milk, either due to latch issues or something else.

- **Baby is crying or in pain after feeding:** If your baby is suddenly crying after feeding, you might think she's still hungry. She might be. However, crying after feeding will burn calories. Your baby will be sleepier and then wake up sooner, needing a quick top off, but doesn't eat a full meal. She then falls asleep again, leading to a snacking routine.

- **Baby spits up:** Babies will burp and expel air. It's normal for a bit of milk to come with it. If your baby seems to spit up everything you feed her, it could be a problem.

- **Baby goes longer than three hours between feedings:** If your baby goes longer than three hours between feedings, you may not be in touch with what baby or you need. Your breasts will fill when it's time for your baby to eat, and if your baby isn't waking on his or her own, you should probably wake them.

Weaning

Weaning is a big deal for babies, and if you're suddenly introducing solids while cutting back on the milk or formula, your baby may resist your attempts. These are some of the most common problems your baby will face when weaning:

My Baby Won't Eat Anything

If your baby is too young to eat solids, they have a reflex that causes them to push the food out of their mouths, known as the tongue-thrust reflex. This will go away with time. If after a few attempts of providing solids, your baby continues to thrust it out of his mouth, you're probably a few weeks too early.

My Baby Refuses the Spoon

If your baby refuses to be spoon-fed, it could be that your baby simply wants to feed herself. This is actually a good thing; your baby is asserting her independence. Of course, it means that

mealtime may be messier and you might wonder if more food gets on your baby than in, but food before 1 isn't strictly necessary from a nutritional standpoint; it's practice for when your baby needs to eat more solids. Encourage independence if you can. Your baby will get it eventually! And, if she struggles with the spoon, you could try giving her small, soft finger foods that she can feed herself.

The most important thing to remember is that this is normal and any pressure you put on your baby to eat is likely to back-fire. Trust that your baby can regulate her feeding, even if you think that she may need help. At this stage, let your baby eat regularly throughout the day; offer food every 2 to 3 hours during the day, so she has plenty of chances to eat. Keep in mind that your job is to put the food in front of her: what she does with it from then is up to her. She will get most of her nutrition from milk and formula at this age, so don't worry about her starving.

My Baby Refuses the Cup

Most babies don't enjoy cups because it's different from a bottle or breast. Continue to offer them cups with spouts or straws in order to help get them used to it. They'll get it eventually!

My Baby is Afraid of New Food

Wariness is your baby's defense mechanism. If he's wary of new foods, he is being cautious about eating something because he isn't sure it's good. If he's particularly cautious, remember that your job is to provide the food; if he doesn't eat it, he at least was exposed to it. Go at his own pace, and don't react to any funny faces he may make.

My Baby Eats Slowly

Slow eating may occur for several reasons. She may not be hungry, or she might be distracted by something else going on. This isn't necessarily a bad thing, and it gives her tummy time to decide it's full!

My Baby Makes a Big Mess

A parent's worst nightmare can be a particularly messy meal that is suddenly everywhere. However, even if you are dealing with this, remember that your baby is exploring. Your baby needs to develop the motor skills to feed herself, but your baby is also having fun, too. Some of it is probably making its way into his stomach. Don't stop and clean up the food every time it's dropped or your baby might turn it into a game.

My Baby's Tummy Seems to Hurt

Shifting from milk to solids can be a bit rough on the digestive system. Some babies have tummy aches as their bodies learn how to process the new food. You may notice constipation as the digestive system adjusts to solids. If it's a short-term fussiness, don't worry about it. If you notice signs of allergies, you need to speak to your baby's doctor.

Stop Baby's Fussy Tummy Troubles

Fussy tummy troubles can be awful. Many are quite normal, but can be distressing to watch. If your baby is suddenly spitting up large amounts of milk, you might be worried, but keep in mind that this is usually not a big deal. If your baby is gaining weight properly, there is probably no major concern with spitting up. If you notice six to ten wet diapers daily, your baby is probably drinking enough.

Reducing Spit-Up

If you want to reduce the number of spit-up driven messes, no one can blame you! Thankfully, it can be managed easily. Consider the following to reduce instances of spit-up:

- Keep your baby upright or semi-upright while feeding.
- Avoid overfeeding your baby.
- Burp your baby regularly.
- Keep your baby upright or semi-upright for 20 minutes after feeding.

GERD

Reflux usually isn't a big deal in babies, as most babies deal with it to some degree. However, some babies feel pain or suffer from medical problems when they suffer from reflux, and they may be diagnosed with gastroesophageal reflux disease (GERD). This can be identified by a noted lack of interest in eating, fussiness while eating, coughing, hoarseness, and failing to gain weight.

When a baby suffers from GERD, acid splashes up from the stomach and irritates the esophagus. As a result, your baby may try to stop the pain by feeding less, arching their backs, tucking their legs up to their tummies, or coughing.

Most commonly, doctors recommend similar steps to prevent spit-up. They recommend feeding smaller amounts more often, burping more often, and in some cases, may prescribe medication, especially if the baby will not eat or is not gaining weight.

A Good Feeding Schedule for Grazing Babies

If your baby is a grazer, he probably wants to get up and go instead of sitting down and eating. Keep in mind that his tummy is quite small at this age, so eating small bites here and there is natural for them. However, grazing can be difficult to balance nutritionally if you're not careful. You must remember to plan her snacks as you would her meal to make sure that she gets plenty of healthy vitamins and minerals.

For example, choose fun, healthy foods like whole-grain cereals, bananas, cheese, and similar foods to help get protein, carbs, and healthy fats into your little bundle of joy. Also, make it a point to sit down and eat with the family at least once per day. Don't worry so much about snacking and grazing early on until around the 2-year mark, at which point, they can be limited to encourage eating meals.

CHAPTER 5 - CARING FOR AND SOOTHING SICK BABIES

It can be difficult to know the difference between a normal spot on your baby's skin and a spot that can be of concern, but here are a few common things to keep a lookout for:

Birthmarks

Most babies are born with birthmarks. They are likely to fade in time, but ask a doctor if you are concerned.

Stork Bites and Angel's Kisses

Many babies have red splotches on their neck, eyelids, or between their eyebrows when born.

These are blood vessels that grew due to hormones in the womb. They fade over time.

Hyperpigmented Spots

These patches are often found in babies with darker skin, though they may appear on anyone. They are dark patches, typically around the buttocks. They usually disappear within two years of birth.

Moles

Moles may be smooth or hairy, however, they generally should be checked by a doctor. Most are benign.

Sucking Blisters

Some babies are born with blisters on hands, wrists, or lips from sucking in the womb. They clear up on their own without treatment.

Blue Fingers and Toes

Newborns are naturally pale, and the hands and feet may look blue, especially when cold.

Bluish lips may not be a problem, but if you notice blueness in the gums or skin around the mouth,

your doctor should be called, especially if there is difficulty breathing or if you've noticed that your baby isn't feeding as well.

Jaundice

Jaundice is a yellow tinge to the skin and eyes, caused by a buildup of bilirubin. This is the substance created when red blood cells break down. It is then taken up by the liver and excreted. However, in the early days, newborn livers aren't fully active yet, causing more bilirubin to remain in the blood and creating a yellow tinge. A little jaundice is normal and not a cause for concern.

However, if the bilirubin production is rapid or the liver is especially slow it may be dangerous. If you notice yellowing of your baby's skin and eyes, consider having them checked by their pediatrician for treatment.

Breathing Problems

Most babies sound a little rough when they're first born. Their breathing may be irregular or shallow, but this is normal. However, if you are nervous, consider calling a doctor to ask to be checked out.

Umbilical Hernias

Umbilical hernias are caused by a small part of the intestine puffing out the navel. After the skin in the navel heals, there is often still a weakened area where the umbilical cord ran. As a result, crying may push intestines through it. These typically close within a few weeks or months. If it is still large around 6 or 8 months of age, surgery may be recommended.

Keep an eye out for a loop of bowel stuck in the hernia, noted by the mass becoming hard and tender. This is a medical emergency.

Undescended Testicles

Testicles form in the abdomen and descend into the scrotum before birth. Some babies are born before the testicles descend. This is usually corrected soon after birth. However, chilling your baby's skin may cause his testicles to withdraw back into the abdomen, the result of a reflex to protect them from damage. If by the time of 9 to 12 months old one or both testicles have never been seen by the parents or doctor, it is important to speak to a doctor. Surgery may be needed.

Startles

Newborns are often startled by sudden movements and loud sounds. Some will be more sensitive to these than others.

Jittery Movements and Trembles

If you place babies down on a flat and hard surface, they will jerk, as a result of their reflexes.

Some babies may tremble as a result of an immature nervous system.

Twitches

Twitching, especially in sleep, is pretty typical. If the twitching continues when holding the limb, it could be a sign of seizures and should be reported to the doctor.

Physical Conditions in the First Year

Babies go through a lot of changes during their first year. If you notice changes in your baby's health, speak to your doctor if you are concerned. The following conditions are quite common in infants:

Hiccups

Hiccups happen regularly in the early months, and even in utero. It's typically not a big deal.

Try burping your baby to alleviate them.

Spitting Up and Vomiting

Spit-up is a small amount of curdled milk that spills out of the mouth. However, when it is forceful enough and in large enough quantities to force the contents several inches, it is vomiting.

Spit-up is caused by the muscle closing the entrance to the stomach being immature. Any pressure in the stomach area, such as jostling, laying down the baby, or even squeezing can be enough to cause spit-up. It happens a lot more in the early months. Some babies do it after every feeding. Others may spit up rarely. This is normal and not of concern unless you notice your baby is not gaining weight, is gagging, or is unhappy or in pain.

Vomiting is not serious so long as it isn't often and the baby is gaining weight well. It may be caused by excess gas, but it may also continue no matter what you do. If your baby vomits an entire feeding but seems happy enough still, don't feed her until she gives you cues. Call your doctor if you notice the following:

- Spitting up with irritability, crying, gagging, backs arching, coughing, or poor weight gain.
- New vomiting, more than once or twice, with a yellowish or greenish tinge.
- Vomiting plus fever or change in activity or illness.
- Vomiting that is concerning to you.

Changes in Stool Color

Stool color will change from time to time, especially when solids are introduced. They may be brown, yellow, or green. Unless you notice black, red, or white, don't be too concerned.

Constipation

Constipation is hard, dry stools that the baby struggles to pass. It may cause streaks of red blood. This is more common with solid foods when the baby's intestines need to learn what to do.

Some apple, prune, or pear juice can help push their bowels along. If it lasts for longer than a week, speak to a doctor.

Diarrhea

Diarrhea may be caused by the introduction of new food, fruit juice, or infection. It's usually mild, with the only signs being looser stool that is probably greenish and smellier than usual. As long as the baby acts well and is playful and urinating as usual, he should be fine and it should go away after a few days. Continue feeding your baby breast milk or formula as usual, and if diarrhea lasts longer than a few days, speak to your baby's doctor.

Rashes

Rashes may appear in several different forms. Always take your baby to see the doctor to ensure it isn't serious.

Diaper rash is a bit of an exception; most babies have sensitive skin and that can cause diaper rashes. Most babies will have some degree of diaper rash from time to time. A great treatment is to let your baby go diaperless for a period of time. Or, switch to washing with plain water and using a protective coating of petroleum jelly or diaper ointments.

Acne

Acne is a common rash caused by exposure to Mom's hormones in the womb. They usually fade away, but may appear again.

They are especially common on the nose, creating tiny white pimples without redness. These are known as milia; they're caused because the oil glands are producing oil in ducts that have not yet opened up. It usually resolves itself.

Erythema Toxicum

Erythema toxicum is noted by red splotches (purplish on darker colored skin) around ¼ to ½ inch in diameter. They often have a small white pimple head. They usually clear up. If they are larger and full of pus, show them to the doctor.

Cradle Cap

Cradle cap, sometimes called seborrhea, is a patchiness to the scalp that looks like crusty, greasy yellow or reddish patches. They may also be in the diaper area, the face, or elsewhere. To treat this, soften the patches with oil, then wash and brush out the scales.

Impetigo

Impetigo is caused by a bacterial infection to the skin. It is typically not serious, but is contagious. It begins as a small blister with yellowish fluid surrounded by red skin. Disinfect clothing, diapers (if using cloth diapers), and bedding. If it doesn't clear up within a few days, call the doctor as your baby may need a prescription.

Thrush

Thrush is a mild yeast infection. It looks like patches of milk that got stuck to the mouth, but it doesn't wipe off easily. It may cause soreness and cause fussiness when nursing. Often, the baby needs to take medication to treat it.

Cysts on the Gums

Cysts on the gums and roof of the mouth may appear from time to time. They often are white and round. They'll disappear on their own.

Blocked Tear Ducts

Blocked tear ducts can cause the impacted eye to water and tear up, especially in wind. You may also notice white discharge in the corner of the eye, or along the edges of the lids. This may keep the lids stuck together in the morning. They usually open up on their own, but if needed, can be treated with a gentle massage and antibiotic drops. If they don't open up, a doctor may do so in a minor surgical procedure.

Crossed Eyes

Eyes should never be fixed in a cross position. It's normal to notice crossing now and then until around 3 to 4 months of age, but after that, even brief moments of crossing should be reported to the doctor. Crossed eyes may result in the brain suppressing the vision of the eye that does not work, causing a loss of vision. The doctor may prescribe glasses or patching to force the lazy eye to work.

Noisy Breathing

Noisy breathing is common and typically not a big deal, but noisy breathing should still be checked by a doctor. It's often caused by the cartilage around the larynx being undeveloped. As the baby inhales, the cartilage is free to flop and rattle, which creates the noise. If it comes on suddenly, however, it could be due to infection, asthma, or croup, and you want to have your baby evaluated.

Breath Holding Spells

Some babies get so angry that while crying, they hold their breath. This causes them to start turning blue. It often scares the parents for good reason! But, no one can hold their breath to death. At the worst, your baby will hold her breath until she passes out, but at that point, her body will breathe for her. There isn't really anything that can be done to treat this and most children outgrow it eventually.

The First Time Your Baby Gets Sick

The first time your baby gets sick is distressing, but often, it's worse for you than it is for your child! You watch your baby suffer and worry that it's something serious. But, rest assured that for most infants, it's nothing to worry about! Your baby will be fine. Knowing what to expect will help you to help nurse your baby back to health in no time.

Expect Clinginess

Your baby is expected to feel uncomfortable when sick. It's only natural that she may want to cuddle more. This is where closeness comes into play! Keeping your baby nice and close will help

her to feel more comfortable. It might be tough carrying her in your arms, but you can use a baby carrier to strap her to your chest to allow extra cuddling without losing any productivity.

Sleep Easy

If you wake up repeatedly to sounds of your baby coughing or sniffling, you're not alone.

However, getting good sleep yourself will help you to help your precious babe get better as well.

Bring your babies to sleep in your room so you can hear them if it brings you more comfort.

Eat Well

When your baby is too young for solids, ensure he gets plenty of breast milk or formula. If he is old enough for solids, try giving him healthy foods like soup. A homemade chicken soup with parsnips, carrots, and herbs can be easily pureed for your baby to sip at, or, for older babies, you may let him enjoy the pieces of soft foods. You can also toss in some noodles for yourself for additional staying power. You need to stay fueled as well to help your baby cope around the clock.

Ask for Help

If you're dealing with a particularly fussy baby, it may be worth asking for help! If you're both tired, asking for a friend or family member to take the baby for an afternoon can help you feel better.

Ten Reasons to Call Your Pediatrician

If your baby looks unhappy, you may be wondering if you're overreacting by calling a pediatrician. Ultimately, if you're really unsure or you have that lingering feeling that maybe you should ask, then call in. It's always better to be safe than sorry.

Your doctor won't be angry if you go in and everything is well; they'll be glad that their patient is okay. However, generally, these are reasons that you should call in:

Fever

While fevers generally are okay, there are a few times when it's essential to call, including:

- Your baby is 3 months or younger and has a temperature over 100.5 degrees.

- Your child has a fever over 105 and is difficult to rouse or has a seizure.
- Your baby has a fever and a stiff neck. This is noticeable if he screams when you try to bend his chin toward his chest.
- Your baby has a fever and is dehydrated.

Respiratory Problems

Many viruses cause wheezing during breathing. However, if he is wheezing and the skin between his ribs pulls in, or if he looks pale or has blue-tinged lips, call your doctor immediately. You may also need to call if he breathes in more than 60 times per minute.

Vomiting

It's normal for your baby to spit up and vomit on occasion, as we've already discussed. However, if your baby is projectile vomiting or the vomit appears to be dark in color, call your baby's doctor.

Dehydration

Dehydration is a cause for concern and is worth a phone call to your pediatrician in many cases. Signs of dehydration include a dry diaper for six or more hours, no tears while crying, sunken eyes, crankiness, dry mouth, and lethargy. Dehydration may cause electrolyte imbalances, which can be fatal, so it's best to call in.

Long-Term Cough or Stuffy Nose

Babies and children catch colds often. However, if a productive cough continues for longer than ten days or seems to get worse, it's best to have her evaluated at the doctor's office. The same goes for stuffy noses.

Head Injuries

Not all head bumps are cause for concern. However, if your baby loses consciousness or shows signs of a concussion or skull fracture, call your doctor or head into the emergency room. Signs to look out for include:

- Discharge from the ears
- Uneven or dilated pupils
- Vomiting
- Lethargy
- Irritability
- Loss of motor skills
- Pallor

Deep Cuts

Older babies that start moving around are bound to get cut and bruised. Most cuts shouldn't be a big deal, but certain ones require stitching to help heal up quickly or without significant scarring. These cuts are worth a trip to the doctor:

- Cuts with profuse bleeding.
- Cuts that don't slow after direct pressure for ten minutes.
- Puncture wounds (such as from animal bites, nails, or sharp, thin objects).
- Jagged edges to the cut that are unlikely to close on their own.
- The cut is deep and on the face or a major joint.

Extreme Changes of Behavior

Extreme causes for behavior are a sign that there's something wrong. Look for the following signs:

- Difficulty rousing your baby
- Inconsolable crying
- Sudden regression in your child's abilities

Rashes

Most rashes are worth a call, especially if the rashes are spreading, itchy, or in spots. It's best to confirm a diagnosis and get a treatment plan. Certain rashes will not heal without the right treatment and they must be checked out.

Seizure

Seizures are terrifying to see. Your baby will likely be tense, eyes rolling, and body moving erratically. All you can do is keep your baby on her side and wait for it to pass. Upon its passing, call your doctor right away if your child has never had a seizure before.

Ten Reasons Not to Call Your Pediatrician

With the times to call your pediatrician out of the way, let's go over several reasons that you shouldn't call for help. This includes the following:

Low-Grade Fever

All fevers in infants under the age of 3 months should be evaluated, but past that point, temperatures usually aren't a big deal. In older babies, slightly over normal (under 101 degrees) usually is not abnormal. If there are no other concerning symptoms, then you can usually wait a few days to see if the fever subsides on its own before seeing a doctor.

Manageable Crankiness

Sometimes, babies are cranky and disagreeable. If you can manage or soothe the baby through rocking, bouncing, or the like, then your baby is probably fine. If you spend over an hour trying to soothe your baby with no results, then calling is a good idea.

Runny Nose

Runny noses and a little cough are usually no big deal. Your baby probably has a cold. Symptoms are likely to abate over time. If after a few weeks, there still is a runny nose, or if the runny nose is paired with struggling to breathe, worrying fever, inconsolability, or other concerning symptoms, a trip to the doctor may be in order.

Mild Lethargy

Mild lethargy is normal, especially if your baby is feeling sick. However, if your baby is difficult to wake, completely out of it, or otherwise showing concerning signs, you may want to call the pediatrician.

Loss of Appetite

Usually, babies should nurse every three to four hours. Formula-fed babies will usually go a bit longer. But, when your baby becomes active and realizes that she can play with things, she may lose some of her appetite because she has better things to do. Alternatively, her appetite may decrease if she's sick. As long as she isn't dehydrated, she's fine.

Increase in Appetite

Increases in appetite are also not a cause for concern. As your baby grows up, he'll want to eat more often and that's okay. He'll let you know when he's full.

Constipation

As babies grow older, they tend to poop more often. However, if you notice that your baby is straining and hasn't been able to go in several days, she may be constipated. Trying to add a bit of juice to her diet or using a pediatric glycerin suppository could help.

Teething

Teething is normal and there is nothing your doctor will be able to do to treat it. Offer some pain relievers, teething rings, and have some patience. It will pass.

Scrapes, Bumps, Bruises

Unless it was an injury listed in the previous section, or if your baby is inconsolable or you fear that there may be a broken bone, you can treat your baby's minor injuries at home.

Mild Allergic Reactions

If you've noticed signs of a mild allergy, such as a reaction to a new detergent on her skin, or you notice that a new food shows signs of allergy such as pinking cheeks, you can simply stop feeding that particular food or using that detergent.

If you notice moderate to severe signs of allergy, such as a full-body rash, swelling in the eyes and lips, or difficulty breathing, you may need to speak to the doctor.

Allergies

Inconsolability can often be related to allergies to foods. It could be that your baby is allergic to something that Mom is eating that is passing through breast milk, or it could be foods that your baby is consuming.

When introducing new foods, they should be given independently for three days to determine if there is an allergy before adding any new foods. The most common allergies, which make up more than 90% of allergic reactions are:

- Cow's milk
- Eggs
- Peanuts and tree nuts
- Fish and shellfish
- Soy
- Wheat

There is little reason to wait before introducing these foods, but make sure you watch carefully to see how your baby tolerates them. Allergies cause the immune system to react to the food, which may lead to symptoms that could, in severe instances, be life-threatening and require immediate emergency intervention.

Your baby may also be intolerant of foods, which do not trigger the immune system, but may have some overlap in symptoms. If you are concerned that your child may be allergic to something, you should have them evaluated by their pediatrician.

Looking after a Sick Child

If your child is ill, make sure you pay attention to her cues. Listen to her. If she doesn't want to sleep, she's probably okay to play. If she wants to sleep more than usual, that's okay too. Consider implementing these signs to soothe your sick baby and get some better rest for the both of you:

- Keep the room airy. You don't want it to be too warm, or she'll probably feel worse. If she's chilly, you can cover her with a blanket.
- Give her plenty of fluid without forcing her to eat.
- Try to encourage quiet resting games to play to keep her engaged.
- Let your child doze off as needed. Now's not the time to be strict about her sleep schedule.

Soothing a Sick Baby

When your baby is sick, you may need some advice about soothing him. There are many ways that you can help gently provide relief to your baby during those tough times.

Nasal Aspirator

Your baby can't blow her nose. But you can suck it out! Bulb aspirators will help vacuum out the snot and clear the pathway so your baby can breathe easily. Just know that your baby probably won't make this easy! Expect some pushback and possibly screams of protest. In my experience, very few babies accept the aspirator easily.

Saline

When your baby is congested and the aspirator isn't doing the job, saline spray works well as well. This can help loosen up dried snot and boogers so you can remove them easier.

Steam

Steam is a great way to provide your baby with relief. It helps to loosen up the snot. You can run a hot shower with your baby in the bathroom if you don't have a humidifier.

Oatmeal Bath

Oatmeal baths can help soothe dry, itchy skin. Buy some oatmeal ready for the bath or grind some oatmeal in a blender and mix in half a cup to your bath. A 15-minute soak will make a world of difference.

Cuddles

Cuddles are perfect for soothing when your poor babe just can't catch a break. All she wants is to be close to Mom or Dad!

Lukewarm Baths

If your baby has a fever, a lukewarm bath can help a bit. Just make sure that it's not too hot or too cold.

Cold, Fresh Air

Fresh air is a great way to clear the congestion and alleviate some of the respiratory distress she may be suffering from.

Back Rubs

Back rubs, especially with rocking and cuddling your baby can help soothe a fussy baby.

Rocking and Singing

Rocking and singing is a great way to make your baby smile and soothe your baby when she's not feeling the best.

Upright Airflow

Holding her upright to let the airflow help is a great way to help your baby breathe better.

Adjusting Needs with a Sick Baby

When your baby is sick, it's best to adjust to her needs as much as possible. This means making sure that you meet her needs on demand, even though that may mean letting go of the schedule for a bit. Your baby isn't feeling well and often that means sleeping at times that you may not have expected, and letting your baby be awake at others. It's only temporary, and right now, healing is what matters the most.

You may also need to take more time comforting your baby. You can't always cure viruses that ail your child, but you can offer comfort as needed. Especially in the evening and at night, your child may be extra unhappy and need your help. You can get back to normal when your baby feels better.

Medication Mistakes

If you need to medicate your child, you'll need to pay special attention. This means making sure that they are getting the right amount. Studies show that more than 80% of parents make at least one mistake while dosing their children. Most are harmless, but some can be dangerous. The most common are:

- **Giving the wrong dose:** Your doctor or pharmacist may provide you with instructions for dosage. If they don't, the medication will have instructions based on the weight of your child. Dose carefully, using the included syringe or medicine cup marked with mL lines.
- **Repeat doses:** Parents often forget when they've dosed their children and give a second dose unnecessarily. Write down the dosing schedule to prevent overdosing.
- **Dosing too soon:** Your doctor will provide you with instructions on how often to dose your child, or you will need to follow the package instructions. Don't dose closer together or exceed dosages.
- **Giving the wrong medication:** Make sure you read the label for the instructions and expiration date

to make sure it's right. You don't want to give a medication that you think will fix one thing that doesn't actually fix it.

- **Giving medication incorrectly:** Most medications are orally dosed, but some may be for dropping in the eyes or ears, or may even be rectally provided. Make sure you know where the medicine goes before dosing.

Treating Common Illnesses

There are several common illnesses that your child will probably get at least once. These include fevers, the common cold, the flu, RSV, ear infections, diarrhea, and conjunctivitis.

Fever

Mild fevers, especially if they aren't causing distress, should be left on their own. They are a sign the immune system is working! If your child seems uncomfortable, dose with Tylenol and encourage fluids.

Colds

Colds are typically treated with comforting symptoms in the ways that have been listed throughout the chapter so far. Avoid using cold meds and provide Tylenol for fever.

Flu

There isn't really anything you can do for the flu other than treating it like you would treat a cold. You can also get your child vaccinated against the flu if they are over 6 months old.

RSV

Respiratory Syncytial Virus (RSV) is typically not a huge cause for concern. Symptoms will let up after a few days, but the cough may last for a few weeks. Use a humidifier and Tylenol to help treat the symptoms.

Ear infections

Some ear infections will clear up on their own, so doctors are a bit less aggressive about treating them with antibiotics. However, it may require antibiotics to clear. In the meantime, you can dose your child with children's Tylenol to alleviate the pain.

Diarrhea

Diarrhea commonly lasts between five and ten days. The most common treatment is to simply provide plenty of fluids to keep her hydrated.

Conjunctivitis

Also known as pinkeye, this virus commonly clears itself. However, if it is bacterial, as is the case with yellow or green drainage, it may need antibiotic eye drops to treat.

Separation Anxiety

During the seventh month or so, you may notice that your baby is more reluctant to go to other people and he may be afraid of strangers. He may protest as you leave the room or at naptime. This is likely to come along with sleep issues.

However, a good routine will help your child to deal with the anxiety. Treat your baby with a bit more patience and make parting a happy, cheerful thing. Let him know you'll be right back and come back as promised.

CHAPTER 6 - YOUR BABY IS
TEETHING - NOW WHAT?

Your child is born without teeth, but before you know it, she'll likely have a full mouth! Taking care of those teeth begins in infancy before they even erupted. Your job as the caregiver will be to take care of your baby through the teething process and after to make sure that she has a healthy mouth of pearly whites, ready to eat. The baby teeth, though temporary, are still incredibly important and you owe it to your child to set her up for success without letting them decay.

I've found that, often, soothing a baby during the teething process involves the Three C's of Contentment. Closeness helps to calm your baby down while following her cues will help you to know what she needs the most. Finally, maintaining a consistent routine can help you to begin the rituals that will teach your child to keep her mouth as clean as possible to encourage healthy growth of teeth in the future.

Teething

Most of the time, your baby's first teeth will come in around 6 months old, though it could be sooner or later. Your baby will likely be fussy and uncomfortable during the time that their teeth are erupting, and this makes sense; they're literally cutting through their gums. It can be incredibly uncomfortable and your baby will look to you to help make the pain go away. Look for these common symptoms:

- **Drooling:** As the teeth start coming in, you'll see your baby drool much more. Some drool more than others. You may notice that your baby is soaked and will need a bib to help stay clean.
- **Teething rash:** The drooling can lead to teething rashes, caused by chafing and chapping. Pat away the moisture and consider using some Aquaphor to protect the skin.
- **Gagging or coughing:** This is one of the most alarming symptoms. Your child may gag at the mouthful of spit, but this isn't really a concern.
- **Biting:** Biting helps to alleviate the pressure of the teeth poking in. They will gnaw on whatever they can to relieve the pressure, which can be an unwelcome surprise for breastfeeding mothers! Offer something acceptable for your baby to chew on instead.
- **Extra crying:** You'll probably notice your child cries

or whines more simply due to the pain. Others may deal with a lot of inflammation of the tender gum tissue. The first teeth usually hurt the most, so expect extra fussiness.

- **Refusing to eat:** The pain of teething can cause your baby to be reluctant to eat. This is normal. As long as your baby isn't dehydrated or losing weight, feed her on demand.

- **Bad sleep quality:** Your baby may start waking up more often than usual because of the pain.

- **Ear pulling or rubbing at the cheeks:** If you notice your baby is furiously pulling at the ears or rubbing at their cheeks or chins, it's likely because the gums ache.

- **Gum hematoma:** A bluish lump underneath the gums can be concerning to notice, but most of the time, it's just a bit of blood trapped under the gums. It's not much of a cause of concern unless it continues to grow.

If you notice that your baby is suffering from a fever, is inconsolable, has diarrhea, or is suffering from a rash, you may want to speak to a doctor to make sure everything is okay.

Soothing a Teething Baby

If your baby is suddenly inconsolable, there are many ways that you can help treat them. My favorite methods of treating a poor teething baby include:

- **Wet cloths:** A frozen wet cloth is a great way to reduce inflammation in the gums while feeling great at the same time. You can also massage the gums with the frozen cloth to help alleviate symptoms.
- **Cold foods:** You may also want to serve cold foods to your baby, such as yogurt, applesauce, or frozen fruits in a mesh feeder for your child to gum at.
- **Teething biscuits:** Between 0 and 12 months of age, you can start offering teething biscuits. Just make sure that you pay attention to oral hygiene and clean the mouth out as you do.

Soothing at Night

At night, if you need to treat the symptoms of teething, you can try massaging the sore gums or offering the frozen wet cloth. If you have a particularly fussy baby, giving her some acetaminophen can help take the edge off the pain so she can sleep.

Also, make sure that your baby's face is nice and dry, and make sure it's not drooling chafing that is causing your baby problems with pain. Nighttime teething problems can be distressing, but remember that your baby is uncomfortable and isn't trying to make you miserable. It's only temporary!

Remedies to Avoid

Though some parents may swear by these methods, there are a few treatments that are simply best avoided. These include:

- **Topical medications with lidocaine or benzocaine:** Yes, these might alleviate pain temporarily, but they offer such brief relief that they aren't really a viable option. Your baby will also be swallowing this medication and getting it into their bloodstream. It's better to avoid this altogether.
- **Certain teethers:** Certain teethers may be filled with liquid, or made of breakable material. These are dangerous for your baby. Frozen teethers may also be too hard for your baby's mouth and can lead to distress. It's better to avoid these altogether. Look for teethers made of rubber.
- **Teething necklaces:** Some people swear by amber teething necklaces, saying that they alleviate the pain of teething. There's no evidence of this being true, and they pose a choking and strangulation risk.

Fluoride

Fluoride helps prevent tooth decay because it hardens the enamel of teeth. It's often added to tap water, but this is not the case everywhere. You will need to check if it is routinely added in your area. If not, your doctor may recommend a fluoride supplement.

Tooth Decay and Bottles

Though your child's baby teeth won't be around forever, they are still important to take care of. Tooth decay in infants is usually referred to as "Baby Bottle Tooth Decay". It is most commonly found in the upper front teeth, but may impact other teeth as well. It's believed that this is caused by babies put to bed with bottles. The formula or milk pools in the mouth and allows for decay to occur.

It can also be passed down from parent to child if the parent puts a spoon or something else in their mouth before sharing with their child. Bacteria in the saliva can be passed on and lead to cavities in the baby as well. You can take preventative measures such as:

- Not sharing saliva with the baby through sharing eating utensils.
- Clean your baby's gums with a washcloth after each feeding.
- Brush teeth as soon as they're present with a tiny

smear of toothpaste (following instructions on the packaging).

- Don't fill bottles with sugar water or juice.
- Don't send your baby to bed with a bottle.
- Encourage using a cup by the age of 1.
- See the pediatric dentist as soon as your baby has their first tooth come through.

Dental Emergencies

Sometimes, dental emergencies happen. Knowing how to handle them can make the difference between saving a tooth or losing it. Consider the following:

Tooth Knocked Out

When a tooth is knocked out, keep it moist. Do not touch the root and place it in the socket if possible. If not, place it between your child's cheek and gum or in a cup of milk and call the dentist.

Cracked Tooth

Rinse the mouth with warm water and keep a cold compress on it to reduce swelling. Call the dentist.

Toothaches

Use warm water to clean out the mouth and use floss to remove anything stuck between the tooth or gum. Don't use a sharp object.

Hygiene

Your child counts on you to keep her mouth clean in those early months and years. Oral hygiene begins shortly after birth, wiping the gums with a moist, clean washcloth or gauze pad. As teeth start to appear, decay may occur. As teeth do appear, make sure you brush their teeth at least twice a day to keep them healthy and clean.

Under the age of 3, children should use a tiny amount of fluoride toothpaste; it should be no larger than a grain of rice. Your child will likely fight with you over this, but you should still make it a point to brush daily. Setting good oral hygiene begins in infancy and will prepare your child for a healthy future!

LEAVE A 1-CLICK REVIEW!

Thank you for your recent purchase. I hope you loved it as much as I do!

Raising babies is work and is the most amazing and rewarding experience a mother could ever ask for.

If you don't mind writing a review, I would love to read it. Your opinion matters and helps me make better books for you to read in the near future. Please scan the QR code to leave your review on Amazon.

FINAL WORDS

When you first become a parent, you're likely to feel confused. Those babies don't come with manuals! It's hard knowing how to soothe them in those early days, but with practice, you can do so. Remembering my Three C's of Contentment will help you to understand the best way to bring calmness back to your household. You will be able to help guide your baby through the formative years by remembering to keep him close, follow his cues, and maintain consistency in routines.

I will never forget the moment when my first child was placed in my arms. I remember the trepidation. The doubt that I'd be able to keep my darling safe and happy. I will never forget my worries that I wouldn't be enough. And yet, I learned something very quickly. I might not have known what I was doing, but I was enough. I was all my baby, and subsequent babies, wanted.

Your baby wants you. Your baby wants to be held close and loved. Your baby wants to be able to feel comfortable and cared for. And you are the right person for the job. You might be learning to parent, but your baby is learning to live. It's a learning experience for the two of you, and you are exactly right for the job. And, in a few years when your baby can talk, he or she will tell you how much you are the best parent. In your child's eyes, you will be the one who hung the moon and stars.

Using the tools provided in this book won't prepare you for every moment, but they will help you to understand and recognize the basics to keep your baby healthy and happy. And anything you don't know yet? You'll learn it in time. Parenting is always a work in progress. You don't have to be the perfect parent; you just have to do what you need to keep your baby happy and healthy. And now, you've got the tools to do just that.

Good luck, Mama or Daddy! You've got this!

REFERENCES

Alli, R. A. (2020, December 20). *Soothing your sick child.* WebMD. Retrieved September 21, 2021, from https://www. webmd.com/parenting/baby/soothing-sick-child#1.

American Dental Association. (n.d.). *Baby bottle tooth decay.* Mouth Healthy . Retrieved September 21, 2021, from https:// www.mouthhealthy.org/en/az-topics/b/baby-bottle-tooth-decay.

American Dental Association. (n.d.). *Concerns.* Mouth Healthy. Retrieved September 21, 2021, from https://www. mouthhealthy.org/en/babies-and-kids/concerns.

American Dental Association. (n.d.). *Healthy Children's Dental Habits.* Mouth Healthy. Retrieved September 21, 2021, from https://www.mouthhealthy.org/en/babies-and-kids/ healthy-habits.

American Dental Association. (n.d.). *Healthy habits*. Mouth Healthy . Retrieved September 21, 2021, from https://www.mouthhealthy.org/en/babies-and-kids/healthy-habits.

American Dental Association. (n.d.). *Teething*. Mouth Healthy . Retrieved September 21, 2021, from https://www.mouthhealthy.org/en/az-topics/t/teething.

Ben-Joseph, E. P. (Ed.). (2018, January). *A guide for first-time parents (for parents) - nemours kidshealth*. KidsHealth. Retrieved September 21, 2021, from https://kidshealth.org/en/parents/guide-parents.html.

Bhargava, H. D. (2020, August 12). *Teething in babies: Symptoms and remedies*. WebMD. Retrieved September 21, 2021, from https://www.webmd.com/parenting/baby/teething-symptoms-remedies#1.

Bielecki, C. (2009, November 3). *Baby feeding Myths every parent should know*. Parents. Retrieved September 21, 2021, from https://www.parents.com/baby/feeding/problems/baby-feeding-myths/.

Carter, Melissa. November 5, M. (2017, April 16). *How to cope and the first time your baby gets sick*. Today's Parent. Retrieved September 21, 2021, from https://www.todaysparent.com/baby/how-to-survive-babys-first-illness/.

Cleveland Clinic. (2021, August 20). *4 ways to soothe your teething baby*. Cleveland Clinic. Retrieved September 21, 2021, from https://health.clevelandclinic.org/teething-101-4-pediatrician-approved-ways-to-soothe-a-teething-baby/.

de Bellefonds, C. (2021, June 15). *When do babies start teething?* What to Expect. Retrieved September 21, 2021, from https://www.whattoexpect.com/first-year/teething/.

DeSouza, L., & Crawford, C. (2015). *Eat, play, sleep: The essential guide to your baby's first three months.* Atria Books.

DiMaggio, D., & Cernigliaro, J. (2020, November 19). *Baby's first Tooth: 7 FACTS parents should know.* HealthyChildren.org. Retrieved September 21, 2021, from https://www.healthychildren.org/English/ages-stages/baby/teething-tooth-care/Pages/Babys-First-Tooth-Facts-Parents-Should-Know.aspx.

Dixon, H. (2016, December 15). *The Comfort Cure: 10 great ways to soothe a sick baby.* Red Tricycle. Retrieved September 21, 2021, from https://redtri.com/bump-baby/great-ways-to-soothe-a-sick-baby/.

Donvito, T. (2021, August 30). *17 ways to Soothe Baby's Upset Stomach.* Parents. Retrieved September 21, 2021, from https://www.parents.com/baby/health/ways-to-stop-babys-fussy-tummy-troubles/.

Gaylord, J., & Hagen, M. (2005). *Your baby's first year for dummies.* Wiley.

The Healthline Editorial Team. (2016, February 16). *Poor feeding in infants: Causes, emergency care & treatments.* Healthline. Retrieved September 21, 2021, from https://www.healthline.com/health/poor-feeding-in-infants#home-remedies.

Huber, Joelene. September 13, J. (2020, September 13). *6 common medication errors parents make with kids.* Today's Parent. Retrieved September 21, 2021, from https://www.todaysparent.com/family/medication-mistakes-parents-make-at-home/.

Kerianoff, A. (2021, January 12). *10 Common Weaning problems & solutions.* Mam Blog. Retrieved September 21, 2021, from https://blog.mambaby.co.uk/feeding/weaning/10-common-weaning-problems-solutions/.

Krautter, T. H. (2006). *When your baby won't stop crying: A parent's guide to colic.* Sourcebooks.

Lavin, A., & Glaser, S. (2007). *Baby & Toddler sleep solutions for dummies.* Wiley.

Mayo Foundation for Medical Education and Research. (2020, December 17). *Infant Reflux.* Mayo Clinic. Retrieved September 21, 2021, from https://www.mayoclinic.org/diseases-conditions/infant-acid-reflux/diagnosis-treatment/drc-20351412.

Mayo Foundation for Medical Education and Research. (2020, January 9). *Teething: Tips for soothing sore gums.* Mayo Clinic. Retrieved September 21, 2021, from https://www.mayoclinic.org/healthy-lifestyle/infant-and-toddler-health/in-depth/teething/art-20046378.

Mayo Foundation for Medical Education and Research. (2020, November 17). *Newborn care: 10 tips for stressed-out parents.* Mayo Clinic. Retrieved September 21, 2021, from https://www.mayoclinic.org/healthy-lifestyle/infant-and-toddler-health/in-depth/newborn/art-20045498.

McDonald Neitz, K. (n.d.). *What to do when baby gets sick: 7 solutions.* Parents. Retrieved September 21, 2021, from https://www.parents.com/baby/health/sick-baby/what-to-do-when-baby-gets-sick-7-solutions/.

Morris, R., & Schlosberg, S. (2020, December 3). *How to deal with your baby's spit-up.* Parents. Retrieved September 21, 2021, from https://www.parents.com/baby/feeding/problems/spit-up-faqs/.

NHS. (2018, September 14). *Looking after a sick child.* NHS. Retrieved September 21, 2021, from https://www.nhs.uk/conditions/baby/health/looking-after-a-sick-child/.

NHS. (2019, February 19). *Tips for Helping Your Teething Baby.* Nhs choices. Retrieved September 21, 2021, from https://www.nhs.uk/conditions/baby/babys-development/teething/tips-for-helping-your-teething-baby/.

Perlman Abedon, E. (2015, June 11). *5 biggest baby Food Frustrations*. Parents. Retrieved September 21, 2021, from https://www.parents.com/baby/feeding/problems/5-biggest-baby-food-frustrations/.

Rocketto, L. (2017, March 2). *10 ways to soothe a sick baby*. TheBump.com - Pregnancy, Parenting and Baby Information. Retrieved September 21, 2021, from https://www.thebump.com/a/10-ways-to-soothe-a-sick-baby.

Smith-Garcia, D. (2021, January 28). *How to soothe a Teething baby at Night: 9 tips and tricks*. Healthline. Retrieved September 21, 2021, from https://www.healthline.com/health/baby/how-to-soothe-a-teething-baby-at-night#perspective.

Spock, B., & Needlman, R. (2018). *Dr. Spock's baby and child care*. Gallery Books.

Stasenko, N. (2015, December 4). *Is your baby refusing the spoon? Here's what to do*. Parents. Retrieved September 21, 2021, from https://www.parents.com/recipes/scoop-on-food/is-your-baby-refusing-the-spo

Printed in Great Britain
by Amazon